STUDIES IN MINISTRY AND WORSHIP

EDITOR: PROFESSOR G. W. H. LAMPE

THE CHURCH'S
UNDERSTANDING OF ITSELF

The Church's Understanding of Itself

A STUDY OF FOUR BIRMINGHAM PARISHES

R. H. T. THOMPSON

Lecturer in the Department of Psychology,
Canterbury University College,
New Zealand

SCM PRESS LTD
56 BLOOMSBURY STREET
LONDON

First published 1957

Printed in Great Britain by
The Camelot Press Ltd., London and Southampton

CONTENTS

5

CONTENTS

FOREWORD

I must have been asked to write this foreword because I am not the Bishop of Birmingham and therefore have no official responsibility for the four parishes which are so searchingly analysed in this book.

Mr Thompson has applied the now much used method of statistical analysis to four Midland parishes, but it is fresh to see this system applied to the actual members of a congregation instead of to the general public, which has figured largely in Gallup Polls and similar surveys. The result is a challenging picture of how much yet has to be achieved before those who actually belong to our congregations realize what it means to belong to the Body of Christ, or find in their churches the satisfaction which perhaps we parsons too glibly claim.

One thing I can vouch for, and that is that the problems raised in this book can be found in the countless parishes situated in similar strata in and around all our great cities. I personally find the factual part of this book more convincing than the conclusions drawn from the facts, but it would be very dull to read a book which merely reflected one's own preconceived notions.

I hope many parsons and lay people who are prepared for shocks will read this book and benefit from it.

RONALD LEICESTER

AUTHOR'S NOTE

THE thanks of the writer are due to the four priests who allowed this investigation to be carried out in their parishes and for the interest they have taken in the work. Thanks are also due to all those who assisted the investigation by allowing themselves to be called on and pestered with questions. That people should have permitted such an intrusion is a constant source of surprise, that they should have rewarded it by showering hospitality upon the individual responsible seems little short of miraculous.

The good intentions of the writer being so much greater than his skill, apologies are offered to all to whom, quite unintentionally, he must have appeared discourteous, tactless, unappreciative, or simply boring.

The survey was carried out with the aid of a grant from the faculty of Commerce in the University of Birmingham.

R.H.T.T.

9

CHAPTER ONE

INTRODUCTION

THE thirty years between 1914 and 1944 have been described by Latourette in his massive work *A History of the Expansion of Christianity*,[1] as one of the greatest eras of Christian expansion. During that period the number of Christians increased, they became more influential and they became more evenly distributed over the world. The disastrous effects of two world wars certainly did much to check the advance of Christianity, but in general, the ground lost in some directions was more than made up for by the gains elsewhere. Paradoxically among the debit items in the balance sheet of progress over this period, must almost certainly be placed the decline in influence of some of the major contributors to that work of expansion—the Free Churches and the Established Church of England.

The aim of this investigation is to try and make some contribution to a more adequate understanding of 'the deeper, underlying, general causes which bring about the unresponsiveness of the contemporary mind to the Christian message'.[2] The words are those of Farmer, who in an excellent article has not only stated the problem of this investigation clearly and concisely, but has also anticipated many of its results as well. The term 'unresponsiveness' has been deliberately used in preference to 'indifference' in characterizing the general attitude towards the teaching of the Gospel. Farmer distinguishes between interest and understanding on the one hand, and the capacity to respond on the other. The

[1] Vol. vii, *1914-1944* (London: Eyre and Spottiswoode, 1945), pp. 3, 65, 410.

[2] H. H. Farmer, 'Fundamental Causes of Failure' in Sir James Merchant (Editor), *Has the Church Failed?* (London: Odhams Press, 1947), p. 46.

heart of the problem lies in the question of response. What is most urgently in need of examination is 'the incapacity of the great Christian verities—even when they are listened to—to "come alive" in the minds of contemporary mankind'.[1] The manifestations of this malaise are legion. At an individual level there is the typical case of the factory foreman who had in the past been a keen churchman; he remains unshaken in his religious convictions, yet now possesses only the most tenuous connection with the Church and a sense of bewilderment at his own defection. The knowledge of the Gospel is there, the interest is there, but response seems paralysed. Collectively the multiplication of such symptoms has had serious consequences for the work of the clergy. One writer whose work brings him into contact with thousands of parish priests, asserted that: 'The older clergy, asked whether, after thirty or forty years of preaching the Gospel, they find the work growing less or more difficult, have, *without a single exception*, declared that it grows harder every year.'[2]

As the value of any definition of a problem rests as much with what it excludes as with what it contains, limits have been set to this investigation in certain directions. First, the 'deeper, underlying' causes referred to, exclude from consideration the intellectual grounds for the acceptance or rejection of Christianity. Such factors have little direct bearing on the immediate problem and in any case the scientific, philosophical and theological movements of the last hundred years have been subject to an admirable review in a recent series of open lectures at Cambridge University.[3] Much more expressive of the intellectual problem as it stands between the Church and the great bulk of the people in whom the Church is interested, is that vague but influential force, the climate of opinion. The mass exodus of elementary school children from

[1] H. H. Farmer, *op. cit.*, p. 48.

[2] W. G. Peck, *An Outline of Christian Sociology* (London: James Clarke & Co. Ltd., 1948), p. 131.

[3] H. G. Wood, *Belief and Unbelief Since 1850* (Cambridge University Press, 1955).

12

the Churches upon the completion of Sunday-school, and the much higher proportion of girls than boys featuring in the confirmation statistics, are phenomena which are unlikely to be explained adequately in terms of the failure of intellectual conviction and the preference for some secular philosophy of life. It is true, of course, that intellectual movements do eventually become a part of the climate of opinion prevailing in society and in this form are relevant to the investigation.

Secondly, although any discussion of remedies for the ineffectiveness of the Church of England usually turns quickly to suggestions for brighter services, more cheering and singable hymns, more homely sermons, warmer and more comfortable churches and so on, very little attention can be paid to these factors in this study. Not that they are unimportant. How far the Church is handicapped by its methods and techniques is a matter of some consequence, yet it is hard to be convinced that it is fundamental in the lack of response to its teaching. Religion has flourished in the past despite draughts, dull sermons and *Hymns Ancient and Modern*. Masterman's analysis of this question is unsurpassed, and although written fifty years ago, it remains most pertinent to the present situation. After mentioning some of the current suggestions for improving the attractiveness of institutional religion, he continues:

'All this would be very relevant if we could recognize large populations with real desire after religious devotion on the one hand, and a Church with a living message which can satisfy this desire on the other. The whole problem would then exhibit itself as a consideration of the method by which the one can be most effectively brought into contact with the other. But the conditions are just the opposite. On the one hand we have masses to whom the spiritual world has no meaning, and from whose lives the very fundamental bedrock effects of religion seem to have vanished; on the other we have Churches whose faith has grown cold, and whose good news sounds far removed from anything approaching the passionate enthusiasm of other Christian centuries. Were this indeed present, the problem of machinery would soon be solved. Preachers would be speaking with a conviction itself eloquent; the services would take on themselves a character of infectious courage; the people would themselves build, as always in the past, edifices reflecting in the very stones the characteristics of their faith; religion would impetuously flood out from their limited spaces into the common ways of men. And until such a wind of the spirit can animate the dry bones of religious organization with some such violent life, all conscious modifications of machinery become but attempts at creating the soul by the body, the artificial galvanizing from without of an organism from which the inner life has fled.'[1]

Thirdly, the emphasis laid on 'general' causes excludes certain individual and personal factors which may play a crucial role in the development of religious belief or unbelief in any particular case. Hart, in his classic work, *The Psychology of Insanity*, cites the case in which the atheistic convictions of one of his patients, a former Sunday-school teacher, could be traced back directly to the elopement of his fiancée with the most enthusiastic of his fellow Sunday-school teachers.[2] The effect on religious belief of the strains and stresses of life, particularly those of bereavement and physical suffering, are beyond the scope of this investigation. The methods of the study are in any case unsuited to the problems of pastoral psychology.

Finally, it is inherent in the logic of Christianity that there should be a point where the unresponsiveness of men to the demands of the Gospel moves from the realm of social and psychological research to that of theology. In Christian doctrine, God is the creator, the initiator, working out his purpose in the lives of men and the movements of history. The initiative is God's and the wind of the Spirit must blow when and where it will. This very tentative inquiry is strictly limited to those aspects of the general problem with which its methods enable it to grapple. Only the most unjustifiable extension of the conclusions beyond

[1] C. F. G. Masterman, 'The Problem of South London' in R. Mudie-Smith (Editor), *The Religious Life of London* (London: Hodder and Stoughton, 1904), p. 210.

[2] B. Hart, *The Psychology of Insanity*, 4th edition (Cambridge University Press, 1955), pp. 71, 72.

the limits set by the evidence could enable it to pronounce on theological issues—indeed, only an unduly exalted view of the significance of the project could entitle it to pronounce on any issues whatsoever.

THE VALUE OF SOCIAL RESEARCH

It is not always realized that some at least of the social and psychological problems of the Church are susceptible to systematic investigation. In this connection Welford has suggested that the work of the Church, regardless of denomination, can very roughly be divided into two parts—the theoretical and the practical. The theoretical part consists of 'the guardianship of a Gospel, of a body of doctrine and of an ever-growing tradition'; the practical part involves 'the proclamation of that Gospel, the teaching of that body of doctrine and the realization of the tradition in a functioning Christian community'.[1] The resources of the Church in scholarship and research are today, as in the past, largely concentrated on the theoretical side—on historical, philosophical and biblical problems. Relatively little attention is given to the practical aspect. What little work has been done in this direction, the report of the Archbishops' commission on evangelism[2] for instance, has for the most part been content to draw on the views of experienced individuals. Objective and quantitative studies are conspicuous by their virtual absence.

It is remarkable what little there is in the way of past work on which this investigation can draw for guidance and enrichment. Setting aside the surveys in which the Church appears only incidentally to wider issues, the fruits of such research during the last fifty years are contained in two small Mass Observation reports, one on contemporary churchgoing,[3] the other on the

[1] A. T. Welford, 'Research Work in the Church—A Prospect', *Hibbert Journal*, vol. xliii, 1944, p. 68.

[2] *Towards the Conversion of England.* Report of a Commission on Evangelism appointed by the Archbishops of Canterbury and York, 1945 (Press & Publications Board of the Church Assembly).

[3] *Mass-Observation Reprints*, Nos. 1-6, 'Contemporary Church-going', 1949.

observance of Sunday,[1] and the public opinion poll data on which they draw heavily. Other than this, one must go back to 1904 and the publication of that invaluable document on the religious life of London edited by Mudie-Smith.[2] Earlier again, was the publication in 1854 of the report of the Government census on religious worship in England and Wales.[3] This last report, associated with the name of Horace Mann, created such a storm of controversy that the experiment was never repeated. The work of such people as Brunner,[4] Douglass[5] and Fichter[6] in the United States is of great value in itself, but not surprisingly, it sheds little light on a problem so intimately linked with English social life and thought.

The explanation for this dearth of research in the field of institutional religion appears to be twofold. First, there is the general lack of interest in religion which has characterized the last fifty years. In his report on *Voluntary Action*, Beveridge pointed out that no less than eight of Charles Booth's eighteen volumes of his London survey (1886–1903) were devoted to 'Religious Influences' and added: 'It is difficult to believe that any present-day survey of social conditions in Britain would give proportionate space to the churches and their influence.'[7] It is certainly true that in the various research reports of the much surveyed city of Birmingham and its environs, the Church and religious needs

[1] *Mass-Observation, Meet Yourself on Sunday* (London: The Naldrett Press, 1949).

[2] R. Mudie-Smith (Editor), *The Religious Life of London* (London: Hodder and Stoughton, 1904).

[3] Census of Great Britain 1851, *Religious Worship in England and Wales* (London: George Routledge & Co., 1854).

[4] E. de S. Brunner, *Tested Methods in Town and Country Churches* (New York: G. H. Doran & Co., 1923); *Church Life in the Rural South* (New York: G. H. Doran & Co., 1923); with H. P. Douglass, *The Protestant Church as a Social Institution* (New York: Harper Bros., 1935).

[5] H. P. Douglass, *How to Study the City Church* (New York: Doubleday Doran & Co., 1929); *1,000 City Churches* (New York: Doubleday Doran & Co., 1929).

[6] J. H. Fichter, S.J., *Southern Parish*. Vol. 1, Dynamics of a City Parish (Chicago: University of Chicago Press, 1951).

[7] W. H. B. Beveridge, *Voluntary Action* (London: Allen and Unwin, Ltd, 1948), p. 224.

are lucky to receive passing mention. The second factor is equally important. The almost complete lack of census data on the churches, religious preferences and affiliations has discouraged much of what might otherwise have been done. This was certainly the case in the inquiry known as the *West Midland Plan*.[1] In the introduction to the social section of the plan, the need was acknowledged to consider health, education and religion—the care of body, mind and spirit; the remaining social needs were grouped together under the heading of leisure. It was also acknowledged that the major factor in deciding on the choice of subjects, was the ready availability of reliable information. Investigations in certain directions had to be abandoned when the information coming forward was found to be unreliable and incomplete. It was inevitable that in the final report, health and education should be dealt with at some length, the various aspects of leisure in more piecemeal form, and religion not at all.

In this respect the Church has been slow to realize that in order to learn from the past and understand the present, it is imperative to have facts supported by substantial evidence. Opinions, however plausible, are not enough. The formulation of constructive policy and the solution of social problems require a basis of relevant and reliable information—this is the work of social research. With all its undoubted limitations, it does offer the Church the means of gaining some more adequate understanding of the impasse which it seems to have reached.

[1] *West Midland Plan*, Advance Edition. Sir Patrick Abercrombie and Herbert Jackson (Ministry of Town and Country Planning, July 1948), Vol. 3.

CHAPTER TWO

METHOD

THE chief difficulty facing any attempt to understand the social aspects of church problems was the almost complete absence of reliable information. There was nothing to build on to and very little with which to build. If there were to be valid generalizations, a start had to be made to collect the necessary data on which the generalizations would eventually be based. To this end a study of four Church of England parishes in the diocese of Birmingham was planned.

The experience of churchpeople themselves seemed potentially to offer a more fruitful starting point for the investigation than the experiences of those outside the Church. Parish congregations were likely to present specific problems of their own and churchpeople are subject to the same general influences which condition belief as those who have no church affiliation. The Anglican Church had the advantage of being indigenous—the intricate product of seventeen hundred years of English history. Bound by the most intimate links to this particular nation, its aim is yet that of the whole Catholic Church. The diocese of Birmingham is one of the most homogeneous in the Provinces of Canterbury and York. It is almost entirely urban and is, therefore, the more characteristic of the Church's problems in a country where three-quarters of the population live in cities of 10,000 or more people. In addition, as the Birmingham diocese was about to celebrate its fiftieth anniversary, it was a particularly suitable time for stock-taking.

In attempting to describe and assess the characteristics of the situation in the parishes, the guiding principle was that insisted upon by Thomas and Znaniecki in their classic study of the Polish peasant—the analysis of social behaviour must begin with a study of how the individual defines the situation.[1] In order to find out how people saw the position within the Church, a programme of several hundred interviews was projected.

A. THE INTERVIEW SCHEDULE

So that the required information might be gathered without taking up an unnecessarily large amount of people's time, an interview schedule was drawn up and tested. (It is printed in full in the Appendix, pp. 99ff.) This shared all the limitations of its kind. Not even careful pre-testing could make all the rough places plain. The schedule consisted of a series of standardized questions, designed to elicit the following information: the make-up of the congregation in terms of age, sex, marital status, occupational status and religious background; the religious beliefs and practices of the congregation, how the individual church member saw the parish, the role of the vicar, his own role in the parish, and whether that role as church member appeared to clash with the expectations of the outside world.

B. THE PROBLEM OF OCCUPATIONAL STATUS

It is generally agreed that, rightly or wrongly, some people are often regarded as being higher or lower than others in the social scale. Indeed, many people seem to have little difficulty in identifying themselves as belonging to the working class, the middle class and so on. This has so many repercussions on the way people behave towards each other that it had to be taken into account. It was thought wisest to avoid the slippery concept of 'social class' and the mass of complications with which Pear wrestled in his recent survey of *English Social Differences*.[2] An index of occupational status seemed most suitable and the classification of occupational prestige developed by Hall and Jones was adopted.[3]

[1] W. I. Thomas and F. Znaniecki, *The Polish Peasant in Europe and America*, 5 vols. (Chicago: University of Chicago Press, 1918-20).

[2] T. H. Pear, *English Social Differences* (London: Allen & Unwin, 1955).

[3] J. Hall and D. Caradog Jones, 'Social Grading of Occupations', *Brit. J. Sociol.*, 1, 1950, pp. 31-35.

Occupational status is of course not the only factor which contributes to the determination of class identification. Both Centers[1] and Warner[2] have expressed the view that occupation is the most accurate single index for its prediction. The occupational rankings used are as follows:

1. Professional and High Administrative.
2. Managerial and Executive.
3. Inspectional, Supervisory and other Non-Manual, higher grade.
4. Inspectional, Supervisory and other Non-Manual, lower grade.
5. Skilled Manual and Routine grades of Non-Manual.
6. Semi-skilled Manual.
7. Unskilled Manual.[3]

With its various elaborations and qualifications, the classification is not quite so arbitrary as this might suggest. It is, however, not free from serious weaknesses,[4] and the results of its use cannot be regarded as more than approximations. Particularly was this the case when there were only the often inadequate occupational descriptions in marriage and baptism registers to rely on. The rating was in all cases carried out by the interviewer, the wife normally taking her husband's rating.

C. THE SELECTION OF THE PARISHES

Two pairs of adjacent parishes were selected for study. Two of the parishes were located in the middle ring of the city; one was Anglo-Catholic and the other was less extreme but firmly Protestant. The second pair of parishes was located in the outer ring; one a settled residential suburb, the other a municipal housing estate. The churchmanship was on the high side of

[1] R. Centers, *The Psychology of Social Classes* (Princeton University Press, 1949), p. 191.

[2] W. L. Warner, M. Meeker and K. Eells, *Social Class in America* (Chicago: University of Chicago Press, 1949), p. 168.

[3] Hall and Jones, *op. cit.*, p. 33.

[4] Cf. A. F. Davies, 'Prestige of Occupations', *Brit. J. Sociol.*, 3, 1952, pp. 134-147.

medium in both cases. The parishes have been given fictitious names, but there have been no other attempts to disguise their identity.

It must be emphasized that these parishes do not, and were not intended to represent the diocese in miniature. Only one of the four parishes could be described as prosperous and there was no old parish church among them with its appeal of charm, atmosphere and strategic position. The parishes were chosen to represent types—the Anglo-Catholic and the Protestant churches fringing the business area of the city, the village now grown into a residential suburb, and the new housing estate. The absence of a central city parish was regretted. The lack of resources made it impossible to interview people scattered throughout the city and its surrounding boroughs.

D. THE DEFINITION OF CONGREGATIONAL MEMBERSHIP

In the Church of England it is by no means easy to determine what constitutes church membership. The position here is confused by Establishment. In the Middle Ages every citizen was automatically a member of the Church. With the development of the Free Churches and the Roman Catholic Church, the problem arose of how far their members, by virtue of being citizens, were members of the Established Church, and how the large number of people were placed who had no effective church connection of any kind, but who nevertheless claimed the right to its ministrations. With the formation of the House of Laity as a constituent part of the Church Assembly, a solution to the problem had to be found in order to determine who was eligible to vote in the Church's system of lay representation. It was eventually decided that persons of eighteen years and upwards of either sex who were baptized and had signed a written declaration that they were members of the Church of England, were eligible for registration on the electoral roll.

There is a further consideration. As Cuber has pointed out,[1]

[1] J. F. Cuber, 'Marginal Church Participants', *Sociol. & Soc. Res.*, Sept.-Oct. 1940, pp. 57-62.

there is no such thing as the 'either—or' proposition of church membership. People do not divide simply into churchgoers and non-churchgoers. It is a question of degree and not of clear-cut lines of demarcation. In order to establish a series of congregations for investigation, it was clear that some kind of arbitrary distinction would have to be made. Michonneau,[1] Fichter[2] and Garbett have all offered fairly similar classifications of the laity. Garbett divided the laity of the Church of England into three groups: (a) 'those who are instructed and convinced Churchmen and Churchwomen', the devoted and hard-working core in every parish; (b) 'the laity who make their Communion occasionally, attend Church fairly frequently and are ready to make their contribution—on a moderate scale—to the funds of the Church'; (c) 'those who call themselves "C. of E.", who claim the benefits of the Church on rare occasions of their lives, but who never attend its services, except on some special day of prayer and praise. They know nothing of its doctrine, worship or discipline; but they would be indignant at any attempt to un-Church them.'[3]

In each of the four parishes a list was made of the 'effective' adult congregation, i.e. all those people eighteen years and over who fell within the first two of Garbett's categories. In practice the list was basically the parish electoral roll with a certain number of additions and deletions. Every member of the congregations interviewed gave an affirmative answer to the question: 'Do you feel that you need some form of religious belief in order to live a full and happy life?' Throughout this report the term 'congregation' will refer to this strictly limited group; the term 'parish' or 'parishioners' will refer to the geographical area or all those living within the bounds of the parish regardless of their religious affiliation.

[1] G. Michonneau, *Revolution in a City Parish* (Oxford: Blackfriars, 1949), p. 9.

[2] J. H. Fichter, S.J., 'The Marginal Catholic: An Institutional Approach', *Soc. Forces*, 32, 1953, p. 167.

[3] C. J. Garbett, *The Claims of the Church of England* (London: Hodder & Stoughton, 1937), pp. 176f.

E. THE INTERVIEWING PROCEDURE

In the parishes of St Matthew, St Mark and St John, every member of the congregation was approached to enlist their support of the project and to make an appointment. In St Luke's parish, where the membership was considerable, every third member on the list was approached in the same manner. The modal length of the interview was approximately one hour and a half. The usual pattern of the interview consisted of an explanation of the project, the specific questions, and general discussion. The answers were recorded immediately. Where husband and wife were both included in the congregation, the interview was carried out jointly.[1] This procedure had definite advantages and caused no noticeable restraint. In a few cases where an interview would have been too difficult to arrange, the schedule was used in its questionnaire form. Altogether 370 people were included in the lists and interviews were completed in all but eighteen cases. The reasons for these failures were as follows: bereavement (1); extreme old age (1); not Church of England (1); ill-health, usually in hospital (5); disinclined to assist or positively opposed (10). The degree of co-operation was a reflection of the concern felt for the situation of the Church.

[1] Cf. J. D. Thompson and N. J. Demerath, 'Some Experiences with The Group Interview', *Soc. Forces* 31, 1952, pp. 148-154. Also R. K. Merton, M. Fiske and P. Kendall, *The Focussed Interview*, *A Manual*, 2nd edition (New York: Bureau of Applied Social Research, Columbia University, 1952), pp. 134-167.

CHAPTER THREE

ST MATTHEW'S PARISH

ST MATTHEW'S is a long triangular parish in the middle ring, stretching along two slightly diverging roads leading away from the city. In 1898 when the church was built, the parish consisted of a residential area for well-to-do business people, its outer boundary verging on what was almost open countryside. Before the 1914-18 war, this was a prosperous parish; it supported a curate and its services were well attended.

The last fifty years brought many changes. The natural course of city expansion took its inevitable toll of the area. The residential seclusion of the parish was invaded by the inner business zones of the city and along the two principal roads, what had once been family homes were increasingly converted into business premises, schools, apartments and lodging houses. This process was accelerated by the 1939–45 war. The original occupants, the supporters of the church, moved further out towards the circumference of the city and their place was taken by new groups of people.

Now a struggling church finds itself situated in the middle of a mixed area of housing, varying from the decayed, overcrowded and squalid conditions at one end of the parish to the modern detached and semi-detached homes of the business and professional people at the other. The population is becoming increasingly cosmopolitan. The proximity of the Jewish school and synagogues has always attracted a large number of the Jewish people to the district and now the overwhelming majority of the newcomers are Irish Roman Catholics, West Indians, Africans and Pakistanis, many of whom are Muslim. Many of these people reside only temporarily in the parish until such time as they can secure more permanent accommodation.

THE CHURCH

The red-brick Gothic church is well sited on a busy highway; its hall and clubroom placed conveniently alongside. The church-manship is firmly Protestant, but not to an extreme degree; it could perhaps be best described as 'medium-low'. Evensong is the principal Sunday service after which members of the congregation are encouraged to meet together over tea. The church remains locked for six days of the week except for such special services as weddings or funerals. Around the church are the various subsidiary parish organizations, the Sunday-school, choir, ladies' working party, men's club, youth club and badminton club. Membership in any of these organizations does not carry any definite obligation to attend church services.

The church has recently been showing signs of growth. Owing to the ill-health and the old age of the previous incumbent, who had been in the parish for thirty-five years, the parish had sunk to a low ebb. Since the arrival of the present vicar, collections, total financial receipts and the number of communicants, have all been doubled. The scope of parish activities has also been widened to include such features as a piano recital of music by Chopin, given in the church, performances by an outside drama group of Eliot's play, *Murder in the Cathedral*, and special services for groups whose sports grounds or school buildings lay within the parish boundaries.

THE CONGREGATION

Table I indicates the make-up of the congregation in terms of age, sex and marital status.

The congregation had certain striking features: (*a*) the high proportion of women; (*b*) the high proportion of women over fifty years of age who were either widowed or single; (*c*) the relative weakness of the thirty to thirty-nine year age group; (*d*) the high age level of the congregation, with more than half aged fifty years and over and almost one-third of the congregation made up of women over sixty years of age.

TABLE I. COMPOSITION OF THE CONGREGATION

WOMEN

Age	Number	Married	Single or Widowed
70 plus	18	1	17
60–69	12	4	8
50–59	10	5	5
40–49	12	11	1
30–39	6	5	1
18–29	14	3	11
Total	72	29	43

MEN

Age	Number	Married	Single or Widowed
70 plus	5	4	1
60–69	4	3	1
50–59	7	6	1
40–49	9	9	0
30–39	5	4	1
18–29	5	1	4
Total	35	27	8

Figure I indicates: (a) the occupational status of the congregation; (b) the occupational status of the fathers of infants baptized at the church during the nine years prior to the investigation; (c) the occupational status of fathers of brides married at the church during the twelve months previous to the study. It is apparent that the congregation was far from typical of the parish as a whole, or even of that far from representative section of the parish who are 'C. of E.' to the extent of wishing their children to be 'named' or married at the church. The dotted section of the figure indicates the proportion of the congregation non-resident in the parish.

Half the congregation lived outside the parish. In some cases this meant nothing more than the fact that the parish boundaries had little significance. More often, loyalties built up from the time when the families had been living in the parish brought people back in support of the church. Such support was, in fact, maintaining St Matthew's. A small group of families, in some cases linked by marriage, whose association with the church dated back more or

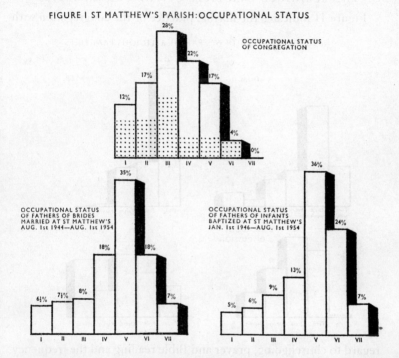

FIGURE I ST MATTHEW'S PARISH:OCCUPATIONAL STATUS

less to the laying of the foundation stone, carried on its work with the aid of a few 'newcomers'.

In response to the question—To what degree was religion an influence in your upbringing?—53 considered that it had been very marked, 36 moderate, 10 slight and one not at all. Forty members of the congregation reported that there had been a time when they had not been active members of the Church of England. The fourteen denominational changes had for the most part taken place during childhood and adolescence and three members of the congregation strictly speaking still belonged to one or other of the

Free Churches. The remaining 23 had lapsed at one time or another as a result of wartime experience, nursing training, illness and so on.

THE RELIGIOUS PRACTICES OF THE CONGREGATION

Figure II indicates the normal practice of the congregation with

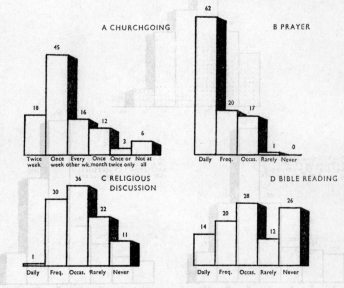

FIGURE II ST MATTHEW'S PARISH: RELIGIOUS PRACTICES

regard to churchgoing, prayer and Bible reading and the frequency with which religious topics were discussed. The most common practice amongst the members of the congregation was to attend one service per week. A small group attended more frequently, usually office-bearers, people with various duties such as bell-ringers, choir members, etc., and some devout women. Old age and ill-health combined to account for those who had not been to church at all.

Four-fifths of the congregation prayed either daily or frequently. No account was taken of the innumerable and all-important subtleties of prayer; with regard to the formality of the practice, those who prayed regularly morning and/or evening were in a minority and usually to be found amongst the higher age groups.

Approximately one-third of the congregation discussed religion with some degree of frequency. Members were divided in their views as to the desirability of the practice; to some amongst the middle and older groups religion was a positively unsuitable topic for discussion.

Teacher in 40's: 'We need to discuss religion freely.'

Clerk in 60's: 'I never argue with people about religion—I don't think it wise.'

Single woman in 80's: 'I can't say we've been very given to talking about religion, we've been brought up Church of England and we've taken it as a matter of course. Those that do discuss religion usually end up with quarrels.'

Approximately one-third of the congregation had some frequent or systematic acquaintance with the Bible apart from church services. Most of these followed the Bible Reading Fellowship notes.

THE RELIGIOUS BELIEFS OF THE CONGREGATION

Figure III indicates the degree of belief in the four chosen points of doctrine. The concentration on two or three adjacent steps of the scale as contrasted with a scatter over the whole range, pointed to the high degree of common acceptance. The greatest agreement was expressed with regard to the existence and Fatherhood of God, and to the Sonship of Christ. The younger half of the congregation tended to be slightly less sure of their convictions.

There was some evidence to suggest that the findings of science were not proving an obstacle to people's religious convictions. Those who saw the religion-science controversy in terms of the doctrines of evolution, determinism, etc., did not feel that science presented a serious challenge to religious belief; this did not mean that they felt there was no tension between them. Others who felt

that the conflict between religion and science was very considerable or even 'irreconcilable' saw the problem in rather different
terms. Science was synonymous with the atomic bomb and was
the villain of the piece. The need was to direct the energies of
science into less destructive channels.

FIGURE III ST MATTHEW'S PARISH:RELIGIOUS BELIEFS

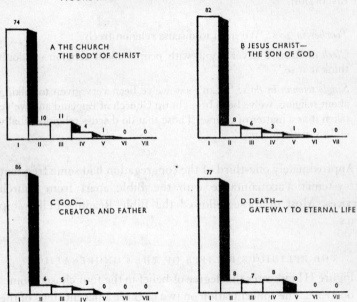

*[The numbers I-VII express the range from untroubled conviction to untroubled
doubt: see Questionnaire, pp. 102f.]*

HOW THE CONGREGATION SAW THE PARISH

There was not one but a variety of pictures of the parish to be
found among members of the congregation depending on the
angle from which they viewed it. The older people were be-
wildered by the changes they had seen in the parish during the
past fifty years.

Widow in 70's: 'I have attended St Matthew's every Sunday
morning since 1919, but there are so few people there now. I think

it is a disgrace—it hurts to see all those empty seats. Sometimes when I get back home I could weep.'

Woman in 70's: 'The parish has been spoilt by a new type of people coming in—Jews, darkies, Irish Catholics.'

The change in the circumstances of the parish meant that more and more work was thrown upon the small hard-working core who consequently tended to become increasingly tired and discouraged.

Housewife in 40's: 'A handful of congregation—the same people doing the same things every week, year in year out—with no new members. There's not much encouragement—there's the support of the faithful only.'

Business man in 40's: 'I know the church has to go on and that some fool has to do the work—but I always maintain that you have to be more than half a fool to do it. The people that really get the most out of church are those that come along to a service and enjoy it and go away without any further responsibility.'

This nucleus of the congregation was divided between those whose allegiance lay primarily with the previous vicar and those who supported his successor; those who distrusted change and those who welcomed it. The younger people were conscious of their differences with certain of the older members. The congregation seemed to them to be divided into two camps—the old and the young—which had little in common.

Those members not carrying the burden of maintenance saw the parish in yet another light.

Widow in 50's: 'A sincere desire on the part of the parishioners of the church to make it spiritually alert and outstanding.'

Housewife in 40's: 'The church is a lively centre with services which are never routine, the sermons and music far above average. Those who like "socials" should be happy in it, for the church halls are constantly used by a variety of clubs and working parties. The enthusiasm of the vicar is hard to resist.'

31

A. THE CONGREGATION AS A FAMILY

In response to the question—Do you feel as though you are part of 'a family of worshippers' at St Matthew's?—71 replied yes, 20 no, and nine were doubtful. A higher proportion of women than men made up the 'no' and 'doubtful' categories, otherwise dissatisfaction did not seem to be confined to any particular section of the parish, though the reasons for it differed from group to group.

Retired woman in 70's: 'I think the people there are cliquey and unfriendly. The only people who ever make an attempt to be friendly are the vicar and his wife. As for the cup of tea in the clubroom, I've gone over there and nobody has said a word to me. At the afternoon gathering I used to go and tried to be friendly, but it was such hard work being friendly that after a while it just wasn't worth it. They don't want you.'

Housewife in 40's: 'No—there is a clique you can't break into.'

Clerk, single woman in 60's: 'Of course I don't know many of the people—you see I'm new to this parish, I've only been here seven years.'

Widow in 70's: 'I've been attending St Matthew's regularly for two and a half years and no one has ever spoken to me yet.'

Widow in 70's: 'I don't feel wanted now I'm old.'

Student in 20's: 'If strictly honest—no—not what I would mean by a family of worshippers. For a time I used to attend a Methodist Church which really was a family—there was a sense of unity every time I was there. This may be due to a lack of my age group at St Matthew's, but I feel there is something lacking in every Anglican church.'

In reply to the question of whether people had ever asked other members of the congregation to pray for them or their family when in sickness or trouble—only 13 replied in the affirmative. Half of the remainder felt free to ask for the prayers of fellow members in the event of future ill-health or trouble; a few others would be willing to ask the vicar.

32

B. THE RELIGIOUS AMENITIES OF THE PARISH

Three-quarters of the congregation felt quite satisfied with the various parish activities as adequately meeting their religious needs. Reasons for dissatisfaction in this direction included the lack of visiting, the lack of friendliness, the lack of week-day services, the lack of devotional and study groups, and the lack of adequate youth facilities. Such dissatisfaction as existed was distributed fairly evenly through the congregation and could not be identified with any particular group, although the grounds for the dissatisfaction varied with the needs of the groups concerned.

> *Professional man in 30's:* 'I should like to see more getting together during the week—talks, discussions, lectures, with special reference to the Bible and Prayer Book. The Lenten services are an opening.'
>
> *Single woman in 70's:* 'The parish needs a women's meeting.'
>
> *Shorthand-typist in 20's:* 'There is not enough done for young people on the religious side of it. The church is run by older people and the younger people don't get a look in.'

Pastoral care in the parish was limited to the conduct of the Sunday and special services, the instruction of confirmation candidates and those intending to be married, and a limited amount of visiting. Only half of the congregation had ever received a visit from the vicar, and of the 47 that had done so, only 18 had been visited in the previous ten months. Many of the visits even then were concerned with the conduct of church business. This was an extremely sore point with all sections of the congregation.

HOW THE CONGREGATION SAW THE WORK OF THE VICAR

Ideally the role of vicar was seen as that of 'friend and adviser' to all. In response to the question of what quality was most to be desired in a vicar, 81 selected the man of great human understanding, 11 the outstanding preacher, two the brilliant organizer and four the man of great sanctity. This last was often received with considerable suspicion and sometimes emphatically renounced.

In general, the work of the vicar was seen as hard, disheartening and underpaid. Occasionally success or failure was felt to depend almost entirely upon the elusive quality of personality. The nature of the specific clerical duties was far from clear in many minds. Some could offer no suggestions as to the tasks inherent in the role of the vicar; others felt that he must be 'ready to do anything' or be 'at everyone's beck and call'.

Two functions of a vicar were in the forefront of people's minds. First, he must be a friend to all. This included all parishioners, churchgoers or not.

> *Student in 20's:* 'Attend to the needs of the whole parish—even the definitely anti-religious. Be a social worker and friend as well as a religious instructor.'

Secondly, he must look after the running of the church. This involved taking the services, caring for the parish clubs and organizations—especially those relating to youth, and building up a congregation. A small congregation was regarded as a reflection upon a vicar and a large attendance at any service or services a matter of congratulation.

The office of vicar, as distinct from the man who held the office, appeared to carry little authority, even in the spiritual sphere. Seventeen members of the congregation asserted that there were no circumstances in which they would call in the vicar, and another 10 qualified their response or asserted that it would entirely depend upon the kind of man the vicar might happen to be. Although 67 included serious illness and death amongst the occasions on which they would call him in, 39 guidance with moral and spiritual problems, and 25 domestic and other problems, there was little indication that theory would necessarily correspond to practice.

As it was usually as a personally trusted friend rather than as one professionally endowed with specific abilities and authority, that people were prepared to consult him, the question of how well the vicar was known to the congregation was vital.

> *Teacher in 40's:* 'On no occasion—until he had made himself a friend, preferably by visiting.'
>
> *Widow in 70's:* 'I don't know—not when I was dying—I might—but I doubt it—you see, I don't know him.'
>
> *Student in 20's:* 'In case of real illness automatically; in case of serious spiritual or moral difficulties after thought and some delay, not automatically. Perhaps there oughtn't to be hesitation but it depends on the type of contact with the priest.'
>
> *Housewife in 20's:* 'Ideally when there is trouble or sickness in family, but it would depend on whether the vicar was the kind of person one could depend on in that way—whether he had a reputation for being helpful in such circumstances.'

With knowledge of the vicar the scope of occasion tended to increase.

> *Housekeeper in 60's:* 'For almost anything if the need was really desperate. He's the first person I'd go to if I needed a friend.'
>
> *Housewife in 40's:* 'Ill health, mental distress and any happy occasion that I thought the vicar would like to be with us.'

HOW MEMBERS OF THE CONGREGATION SAW THEIR ROLE IN THE PARISH

Except in the case of a small minority, the Church was not seen as an institution which made demands upon its members. There were certain things which were 'done' of course, such as leading a decent life and going to church when one could.

> *Civil servant in 60's:* 'I attend St Matthew's when convenient and greatly admire the vicar.'

Fifty-nine people stated that they were aware of rules which the

Church of England expected its members to observe, 41 felt that there were none or were doubtful.

Widow in 80's: 'You have to make your own rules.'
Housewife in 40's: 'There are no rules laid down. It is the great joy of religion that there are no rules. Members are expected to fulfil certain duties such as regular church attendance and bringing up the younger generation in the faith.'
Housewife in 30's: 'Regular attendance at church; good moral behaviour towards one's fellows and doing a little more than one is obliged.'
Clerk in 40's: 'No—there are services you can go to and you give money when you can.'

The church was seen neither as a fellowship nor as making demands upon its members in that direction. Fellowship was an optional extra for those who might want it, but in no way was it thought integral to the process of worship.

Housewife in 40's: 'I go to church to worship God—but I keep clear of the social side of the church. They're all the time squabbling among themselves.'
Housewife in 50's: 'I suppose it is my High Church training, but I do not want to go over to the church room after the service for a cup of tea and mix socially with the people at church. It's wrong of me I suppose.'
Shopkeeper in 60's: 'We like to go to church to worship God in our own quiet way. We do not want to get mixed up with any of the church activities.'

The parish was in great need of extra assistance in the onerous work of church maintenance. Very little use, however, was being made of the resources which appeared to be at the church's disposal. In a hypothetical situation, 28 members of the congregation were willing, if necessary, to conduct matins and evensong, say a 'few words' by way of a sermon and carry out pastoral visiting. A further eight were prepared to do all but say the 'few words'. Thirty-eight members expressed their willingness to join a parish study group in order to learn more of their faith and the Bible; 24 felt that not only could they be doing more to serve the church, but that there was no material barrier in their circumstances to prevent them doing so at once. There were of course many others who would have liked to do more for the church had time, a young family, ill-health or other factors permitted. Those who felt that they could be doing more than they were, explained their position in a variety of ways— the work they were already doing seemed wasted; the matter had never been given any thought; they did not feel welcome in the congregation; and most frequently of all they didn't know what to do.

HOW MEMBERS OF THE CONGREGATION SAW THEIR POSITION IN A SECULAR WORLD

There was little apparent awareness on the part of the congregation of any difference in practice between the values and behaviour of those outside the Church and those inside. Only 10 members felt that there were at least rare occasions when their religious beliefs marked them off from those who didn't share them. Such awareness didn't necessarily cause embarrassment, nor was such experience related to people's capacity to mix with their fellows.

Asked whether people had met situations in which the behaviour they thought right for themselves as Christians had clashed with the expectations of their friends and associates, 14 were aware of having met instances where religious principle and group loyalties conflicted. In contrast to this, all were at once conscious of being embarrassed when having to decide whether to continue to say grace, kneel to pray or observe the Lenten discipline when in the presence of non-churchpeople or people who might possibly have no church affiliation. In such situations as this, people felt considerable pressure to conform to the general practice of the non-churchgoing. The majority were determined that in such situations they would not alter their general practice. In fact, however, the saying of grace, the practice of kneeling to say private prayers and the observance of Lenten discipline had ceased with all but a small minority.

CHAPTER FOUR

ST MARK'S PARISH

ST MARK'S is a diminutive parish in the middle ring of the city
—less than half a mile long and only a quarter of a mile across at
the widest point. Promoted to the status of a parish in 1903, it had
until that time been a mission for its mother church which was
barely one hundred yards away. Adjacent to the blighted section
of St Matthew's parish, it differs from St Matthew's in that the
progressive process of deterioration which had affected only one
portion of that parish, has in St Mark's become a completed and
established fact.

The parish is a small section of a blighted part of the city
scheduled for eventual redevelopment. This area is largely one of
business premises and light manufacturing industries mixed in
with the remnants of a residential section of an older and smaller
city which has been engulfed by commercial expansion. The
general state of housing decay in this factory-business-residential
area is unredeemed even by such euphemistic names as 'Belle Vue'.
The narrow streets are badly lit and badly paved, the only open
spaces the rubble-strewn bomb-sites on which children play
regardless of the film of mud which covers the place through the
winter months.

This is an area in which much is transitory. A constant flow of
new arrivals—Africans, Pakistanis, Irish and West Indians—has
displaced the former residents and church supporters who have
moved into the outer zones of the city. Here are to be found the
overcrowded settlements of foreign-born populations drawing
references to the 'coloured quarter' and the 'Burma Road'; here
also is a mushroom growth of boarding-houses.

THE CHURCH

St Mark's Church is tucked inconspicuously away in a side street. There is a more or less continuous line of building from the church, church school and hall to adjoining houses, so that it is not easy to recognize it as a church at all. Inside the building, however, there is no mistaking its purpose. The rood above the screen, the tall candles on the high altar, the stations of the cross, the statues of the patron saint and the Blessed Virgin with candles burning before them and the screened chapel for the perpetual reservation of the sacrament, proclaim its doctrinal allegiance. The churchmanship is Anglo-Catholic of an extreme variety.

Mass, preceded by Matins, celebrated daily at an early hour, Evensong said daily in the church, Devotions and an afternoon gathering for mothers make up the regular week-day services. High Mass on Sunday is the principal service of the week, for which the congregation turns up in force together with a large body of children from the parish.

In one respect the recent history of the parish has been unusual. Under its previous vicar, St Mark's had been for a long period one of the 'rebel' parishes. This episode in diocesan history had arisen out of the refusal of 15 beneficed priests to accept the conditions under which the late Bishop of Birmingham had been prepared to take no action regarding the reservation of the sacrament. As a result, St Mark's together with the other parishes concerned, had to all intents and purposes ceased to have any dealings with the remainder of the diocese.[1] This event still coloured the thinking of some of its members.

The church school provides the congregation with virtually its only contact with the parish. Most of the clubs or organizations, apart from those designed to assist the conduct of the services, are

[1] Cf. the pamphlet by S. A. King, *Obedience in the Diocese of Birmingham* (Birmingham: The Midland Educational Co. Ltd., 1926), p. 19; and G. D. Rosenthal and F. G. Belton, *So-called Rebels: A Record of Recent Events in the Diocese of Birmingham* (London: A. R. Mowbray, 1930).

ST MARK'S PARISH

designed for youth and of a social nature. There is no social or devotional group for adults. All church organizations and activities are closed to any but regular worshippers at the church. This rule is enforced so rigidly that even prominent members of the congregation cannot bring their husbands or wives to such functions as the parish supper if for some reason or other they are not regular worshippers. The great majority of the congregation viewed this restriction as unnecessary.

THE CONGREGATION

Table II indicates the make-up of the congregation in terms of age, sex and marital status.

TABLE II. COMPOSITION OF THE CONGREGATION

WOMEN

| Age | Number | Marital Status | |
		Married	Single or Widowed
70 plus	10	3	7
60–69	9	1	8
50–59	8	3	5
40–49	19	13	6
30–39	4	2	2
18–29	6	1	5
Total	56	23	33

MEN

Age	Number	Married	Single or Widowed
70 plus	1	1	–
60–69	1	–	1
50–59	2	2	–
40–49	8	8	–
30–39	3	3	–
18–29	6	1	5
Total	21	15	6

The congregation showed certain significant features: (*a*) the high proportion of women amounting to almost three-quarters of the congregation; (*b*) the single or widowed status of the majority of the women; (*c*) the relative weakness of the thirty to thirty-nine age group; (*d*) the high age level of the congregation with more than half the members of fifty years and over.

FIGURE IV ST MARK'S PARISH: OCCUPATIONAL STATUS

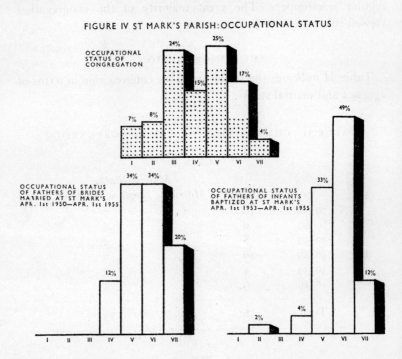

Figure IV indicates: (*a*) the occupational status of the congregation; (*b*) the occupational status of the fathers of infants baptized at the church during the two years prior to the investigation; (*c*) the occupational status of the fathers of brides married at the church during the five years previous to the study. In terms of occupational status, the congregation was not representative even of the highly select group within the parish which did make use of the occasional offices of the church. The dotted section of the figure indicates the proportion of the congregation non-resident in the parish.

Six out of every seven members of the congregation lived outside the parish. This was not the case twenty or even ten years earlier. The majority of the present congregation had grown up in and around the parish—had been educated and made their friends in the church and school. Marriage and the need for accommodation, or simply the general exodus towards pleasanter residential areas had scattered the congregation across three parts of the city, and even beyond its borders altogether. The mere process of going to church involved some in a journey lasting as much as an hour.

Friendships within the congregation were largely determined in terms of the usual age groupings and family relationships. Since the dispersion, however, distance had largely limited visiting amongst the congregation to members of the family and friends who at least lived in the same general direction. Certain key-households were exceptions to this and played a valuable role in uniting the parish. Combining remarkable qualities of personality, and homes in fairly strategic positions, these people provided valuable meeting points, knowing and visiting most other members and being visited in turn.

To the question of what influence religion had had in childhood —47 considered that it had been very marked, 16 moderate, nine slight and two none at all. Nine members of the congregation had at some stage of their lives belonged to other denominations, and three others had had no religious affiliation. Eight members of the congregation had at some period of their lives, as the result of war experience, the care of young children, etc., ceased to have any active connection with the church. Marriage was the greatest single factor responsible for bringing into the church those without a religious background or bringing about a change in denominational allegiance.

THE RELIGIOUS PRACTICES OF THE CONGREGATION

Figure V describes the frequency with which the practices of churchgoing, prayer and Bible reading were observed and the frequency with which religious topics were discussed.

Normal churchgoing extended in the case of some individuals to as many as six or seven services a week. The modal practice of

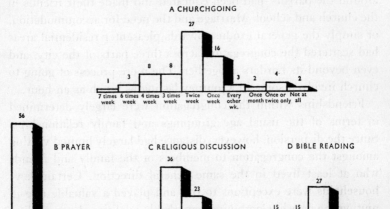

FIGURE V ST MARK'S PARISH: RELIGIOUS PRACTICES

the congregation was twice a week despite the very considerable distances which many had to travel to church. Prayer in some form was the daily practice of the great majority of the congregation, but frequent or systematic Bible reading was confined to considerably less than half of the members. Religion formed a relatively frequent topic of discussion though some members felt that it was unwise.

THE RELIGIOUS BELIEFS OF THE CONGREGATION

Figure VI indicates the degree of belief in the four chosen points of doctrine. There was a remarkable degree of conformity with regard to these points. Such scatter as did exist was provided by the youngest age group, especially in the first and last items. The question of death and eternal life seemed remote to them.

Science did not appear to be disturbing to religious belief. To a third of the congregation the question had no meaning. To the half that saw the problem in terms of evolution, for example, there appeared to be nothing in science which reduced religion to irrationality even though it might raise difficult problems. The

FIGURE VI ST MARK'S PARISH: RELIGIOUS BELIEFS

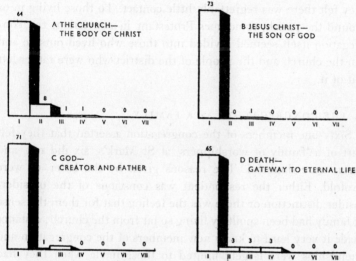

[*The numbers I-VII express the range from untroubled conviction to untroubled doubt: see Questionnaire, pp.* 102 *f.*]

remaining members saw the issue in terms of the atomic bomb, with science as the villain.

HOW THE CONGREGATION SAW THE PARISH

There was a sense of awareness in the congregation that St Mark's stood for something special, an awareness which the years as 'rebels' no doubt did little to diminish. The church commanded great loyalty and affection, especially amongst the older members and those who had received their education at the church school.

Although clashes of personality amongst those who maintained the considerable voluntary work of the church were not entirely unknown, the congregation was remarkably united. One division, however, was evident; it cut deep although crossed by mutual loyalties and friendships. This was the division between those living within the parish and its surrounding district and those living outside. To those living outside, Anglo-Catholics by conviction, there was on the one hand the congregation and on the other hand the parish in which the church was situated, between which they felt there was regrettably little contact. To those living in or around the parish, sometimes Protestant in conviction, the congregation itself seemed divided into those who lived outside and ran the church and the people of the district who were rather left out of it.

A. THE CONGREGATION AS A FAMILY

Sixty-one members of the congregation asserted that they felt part of a 'family of worshippers' at St Mark's, six did not, and seven were doubtful. The reasons given by the latter 13 were twofold. Either the respondent was conscious of the outsider/insider distinction or there was the feeling that for them the sense of family had been spoilt by living so far from the church; distance made it very hard to know new members of the congregation and friendships were largely limited to those made when they had lived nearer the parish.

> *Clerk in 40's:* 'Well, of course I've known the people at the church all my life.'
> *Housewife in 70's:* 'Oh yes—my home I call it.'
> *Widow in 70's:* 'We are so much of a family—if we know of anyone ill we pray for them and feel it very much—we don't wait to be asked.'
> *Civil Servant in 30's:* 'I found the people at St Mark's stand-offish. I went for four weeks before anyone spoke to me. You have a terrific job to try and break into the group.'

A further indication of the family atmosphere can be gained from the willingness of people to ask the support in prayer of the others in times of trouble. Thirty-two members had at sometime asked others to pray for themselves or their family; 42 had not.

> *Widow in 80's:* 'Yes—we really are wrapped up with the others—their joys are our joys and their sorrows our sorrows.'
>
> *Housewife in 40's:* 'I wasn't given the chance to ask—people told me they were praying for me.'

Of the 42 who had not asked, 31 felt free to do so should trouble of any kind arise, 10 did not feel free to do so and one was doubtful.

B. THE RELIGIOUS AMENITIES OF THE PARISH

Faced with the question of whether the parish activities of St Mark's satisfactorily met their religious needs—62 answered yes, eight no, and four were doubtful. Most people were aware of an embarrassing number and variety of services—many of which they could not hope to attend. Apart from this aspect of the church, it was felt by some that in other directions the parish activities did fall short of what was required. The most frequent regret was for the lack of Bible study and discussion groups for both youth and adults. Other lacks were more varied and included the lack of service and 'outgoingness' towards the parish and the lack of social activities for the middle-aged.

The pastoral care of the parish was carried out through a variety of means. Frequent services covered most occasions at times when people were most likely to be able to attend, i.e. early morning and evening; the use of auricular confession gave considerable opportunity for spiritual guidance; and regular visiting ensured that the congregation knew their priest. Only two members of this extremely scattered congregation had not been visited by the priest and of the 72 who had, 67 had been visited in the previous two or three months—in many cases more than once.

> *Widow in 70's:* 'If we're away twice then he knows that something is wrong and comes to see us.'
>
> *Housewife in 70's:* 'When I was ill he came every other day.'

HOW THE CONGREGATION SAW THE WORK OF THE VICAR

In response to the query as to the quality most to be desired in the vicar of the parish—60 selected the man of great human understanding, 11 the man of great sanctity, two the organizer and one the preacher. The most striking feature was the general lack of suspicion aroused by sanctity—it had a positive value. Indeed several of those who finally cast their votes for the man of great human understanding did so despite their personal preference for the man of great sanctity, because they thought it would be best for the parish.

Again the work of the priest was seen as hard, disheartening and underpaid, but in this case redeemed by his enormous privileges in the celebration and administration of the sacraments. The congregation as a whole had definite ideas on the responsibilities of a vicar, some having an almost extensive knowledge of clerical duties.

> *Housewife in 40's:* 'Take services; administer the sacraments; appoint suitable people to organize the social side of the church; teach the Faith; visit; extend the influence of the church in the parish and give spiritual help individually; keep the parish in touch with the diocese.'
>
> *Clerical worker in 40's:* 'See that mass is said daily; take communion to the sick; attend to the spiritual needs of the congregation and as far as possible of all the parish; say the daily offices; teach scripture in the school if there is one; attend to the general running of the parish; take part in the church social activities; train candidates for confirmation; preach and administer the sacraments.'
>
> *Shop assistant in 20's:* 'Visiting the sick and the parish in general; taking services; hearing confessions; general oversight of the church organizations; teaching in school if there is one; administration of the sacraments; preparing people for confirmation.'

Such duties were seen in the light of obligations which had to be fulfilled if the priest was to be faithful to his calling. The success or failure of the vicar tended to be judged more on this quality of faithfulness than on the numbers attending his services.

The congregation in general seemed to think of the role of the vicar in terms of three functions in the following order of importance. First, he must conduct the services and, more specifically, administer the sacraments; secondly, he must be a friend and spiritual father not only to the congregation but to all parishioners; thirdly, he must maintain the church as an institution.

Amongst the congregation the office of vicar was not without spiritual authority. He was in the minds of a large section of the congregation their 'Father in God'. This spiritual authority was sometimes attributed only to priests of the Anglo-Catholic persuasion. Only two members would not call in the parish priest under any circumstances; 70, that is almost the entire congregation, would call him in in case of serious illness or death, 39 would call him in for guidance in dealing with moral or spiritual problems, and 41 for guidance on occasions of domestic or other trouble. Many of the congregation were quite definite as to the purpose for which the priest was desired. He was called in as a specialist— to have the benefit of his prayer or advice, to receive from him the sacraments of Holy Communion or Unction.

HOW MEMBERS OF THE CONGREGATION SAW THEIR ROLE IN THE PARISH

The congregation at St Mark's was taught quite specifically that the Christian religion involved certain definite obligations on the part of its members. It was asserted that these were laid by the Church upon her members both 'to protect her own spiritual life and to protect the religion of the weaker brethren'. These rules were presented as the minimum and their mere observance as 'something less than our Lord claims from his disciples'. A service based on love, not obligation, was the ideal. Nevertheless, on these terms, absence from mass on Sundays and other days of obligation and the failure to make use of the sacraments at the appropriate occasions was not mere backsliding but mortal sin.

In reply to the question as to whether there were any rules which the Church of England expected its members to observe,

54 answered yes, 17 no and three were doubtful. How many of the negative and doubtful responses were due to a lack of awareness of the teaching of St Mark's and how many were due to members' identification with the Catholic Church in contrast to the Church of England, is not clear. Almost entirely did the rules mentioned concern attendance at services and the use of the sacraments. The following illustrated the kind of rules which rose spontaneously in the minds of some of the more devout members of the congregation when faced with such a question.

> *Housewife in 40's:* 'Attend mass on Sundays and days of obligation; confession at least once a year; Holy Communion at least three times a year; keep the days of fast and abstinence; almsgiving; keep the marriage vow.'
>
> *Clerk in 60's:* 'Observe festivals and saints' days; keep the fasts—Fridays, days of abstinence, Ember and Rogation days and the eves of the festivals; Holy Communion three times a year; observe the days of obligation; no divorce; make use of the sacraments; make use of confession.'

Although a large proportion of the congregation was involved in one or other aspects of church activity, there yet existed a reserve of people who would have liked to do more and felt that they could. The explanations given for this were various: members had volunteered to do jobs and their offers had been ignored; members had been hesitant lest they offend people who had the responsibility for seeing that certain types of work were done; members could not think what more to do other than attend church more frequently; and finally, the kind of thing members would like to do, such as visiting or working in a team for the sick and elderly of the parish, did not fit into the framework of present parish activities.

HOW MEMBERS OF THE CONGREGATION SAW THEIR POSITION IN A SECULAR WORLD

About one-third of the congregation of St Mark's was conscious of occasions when their religious beliefs marked them off from those who didn't share them; of pressures which made it more difficult to live the kind of Christian life that they would like; and of occasions when they were faced with a conflict of loyalties between the expectations of their friends and the demands of their principles. Instances most often cited occurred in business or factory life.

> *Machine Operator in 40's:* 'You notice the difference in friends at work. They don't cut you but they sneer.'
> *Factory worker in 40's:* 'Yes—people do take it out of you some-times, especially in the factory, but it doesn't embarrass you.'

Several members of the congregation were more conscious of the difference between the Catholic and Protestant sections of the Anglican Church than they were of any distinction between the Church and the world. In some cases both differences were felt.

> *Secretary in 40's:* 'Our particular church makes you conscious not only of the distinction between the Church and the world, but also between low and high church.'

Whether or not people were aware of the pressure to conform to the ways of the secular world, they all recognized the difficulty of having to decide whether or not to say grace, kneel to pray or maintain Lenten discipline in the presence of those who were not, or might not be churchpeople. With certain exceptions, the reac-tions were much the same as in the previous parish. The impression was, however, that a rather larger section of the congregation did in fact observe these practices.

CHAPTER FIVE

ST LUKE'S PARISH

ST LUKE'S is a large residential suburban parish in the outer ring of the city. In 1865 when the parish was formed, the church served a small country village. By the time of the first World War the position had not materially altered. The people of the village worked in one or other of the near-by factories, and apart from some large gentlemen's houses on the main road, the greater part of the parish consisted of open countryside. In the twenty years between the two world wars extensive building schemes changed the face of the parish. The suburb offered to those who were being forced from the centre of the city by the increasing demands of the commercial and industrial world the advantage of the city without the smoke, noise and congestion. Now little land remains free for development.

THE CHURCH

The attractive grey stone church is set back some fifty yards from the main road to which it is linked by a long drive. The church hall is about half a mile away in the middle of the village, and between the two is the church school. The churchmanship has undergone various changes in the past, reflecting the views of the various incumbents; it can now be described as 'medium-high'. Daily Evensong and three services of Holy Communion are the regular week-day services. On Sunday as far as attendance is concerned, honours are fairly evenly distributed between the Communion service, the Family service and Choral Eucharist in the morning and Evensong at night. There are in fact almost four separate congregations.

Attached to St Luke's is a mission church in a more distant part of the parish. This has a life of its own quite separate from that of the mother church. Indeed its corporate life is a great deal more pronounced for its size than in St Luke's itself, and the provision for adult study and social groups considerably more comprehensive.

THE CONGREGATION

Table III indicates the make-up of the congregation in terms of age, sex and marital status. In the other three parishes this table includes the entire list of people whether or not they were able or willing to co-operate in the investigation. Here it merely includes the sample of the congregation which was interviewed. The sample

TABLE III. COMPOSITION OF THE CONGREGATION

WOMEN

Age	Number	Marital Status Married	Single or Widowed
70 plus	4	1	3
60–69	10	4	6
50–59	20	10	10
40–49	11	7	4
30–39	8	4	4
18–29	13	5	8
Total	66	31	35

MEN

Age	Number	Married	Single or Widowed
70 plus	–	–	–
60–69	3	3	–
50–59	4	4	–
40–49	9	9	–
30–39	6	6	–
18–29	7	3	4
Total	29	25	4

53

consisted of every third name on the congregation list. Those who for one reason or another declined or were unable to help were almost all women, were evenly distributed through the strata of occupations and were weighted towards the higher age groups.

The most striking features revealed were: (*a*) the high proportion of women; (*b*) the single or widowed status of more than half the women; (*c*) the more even distribution through the age groups.

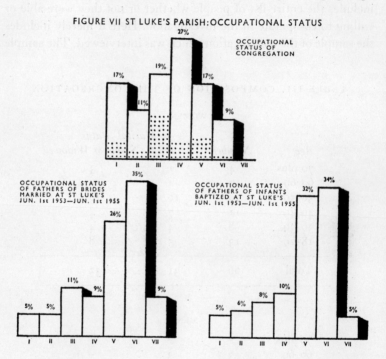

FIGURE VII ST LUKE'S PARISH:OCCUPATIONAL STATUS

Figure VII indicates: (*a*) the occupational status of the congregation; (*b*) the occupational status of the fathers of infants baptized at the church during the previous two years; (*c*) the occupational status of the fathers of the brides married at the church during the two years prior to the study. The dotted section of the figure indicates the proportion of the congregation non-resident in the parish. The congregation was far from representing the parishioners who made use of the services of the church. Even with the addition of the mission church the congregation was substantially weighted in the direction of those who lived in 'more comfortable circumstances'.

One-quarter of the sample lived outside the parish boundaries. This could be accounted for largely in terms of old loyalties, but the charm of its church building and disputes in neighbouring parishes also played a part.

The religious background of the sample was substantial—all but four considered theirs to have been moderate or very marked in influence. Less than a quarter of the sample had lapsed from the Church of England or had been members of other denominations during their lifetime. Thirteen of these had changed in adult life, one from the Roman Catholic and twelve from the Free Churches. Almost all these changes had taken place at marriage, the woman usually changing to the religious affiliation of the man, unless he was unhappy in his own church. The lapses were due to such factors as the care of young children, rebellion in adolescence or bereavement.

THE RELIGIOUS PRACTICES OF THE CONGREGATION

Figure VIII indicates the normal behaviour of the congregation with regard to churchgoing, prayer and Bible reading, and the frequency with which religious topics were discussed. The most common practice was to attend church once a week and to pray daily in some form. Almost half the sample read their Bibles regularly or at least frequently; this was largely the result of the wide distribution of Bible Reading Fellowship notes.

THE RELIGIOUS BELIEFS OF THE CONGREGATION

Figure IX describes the degree of belief in the four chosen points of doctrine. There was the usual high degree of conformity with regard to these points. Such scatter as could be found was largely

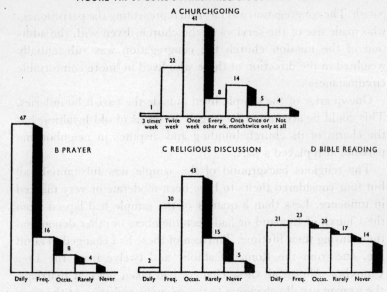

FIGURE VIII ST LUKE'S PARISH: RELIGIOUS PRACTICES

A CHURCHGOING

3 times' week	Twice week	Once week	Every other wk.	Once month	Once or twice	Not at all
1	22	41	8	14	5	4

B PRAYER

Daily	Freq.	Occas.	Rarely	Never
67	16	8	4	

C RELIGIOUS DISCUSSION

Daily	Freq.	Occas.	Rarely	Never
2	30	43	15	5

D BIBLE READING

Daily	Freq.	Occas.	Rarely	Never
21	23	20	17	14

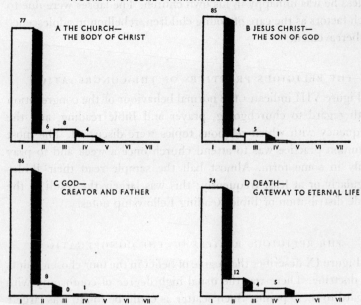

FIGURE IX ST LUKE'S PARISH: RELIGIOUS BELIEFS

A THE CHURCH—
THE BODY OF CHRIST

I	II	III	IV	V	VI	VII
77	6	8	4			

B JESUS CHRIST—
THE SON OF GOD

I	II	III	IV	V	VI	VII
85	4	5	1			

C GOD—
CREATOR AND FATHER

I	II	III	IV	V	VI	VII
86	8	0	1			

D DEATH—
GATEWAY TO ETERNAL LIFE

I	II	III	IV	V	VI	VII
74	12	4	5			

[*The numbers I-VII express the range from untroubled conviction to untroubled doubt: see Questionnaire, pp. 102f.*]

contributed by the younger half of the sample and arose in connection with the questions of life after death and the nature of the church.

As in the other three parishes, the findings of science provided no specific threat to religious belief.

HOW THE CONGREGATION SAW THE PARISH

The congregation was very conscious of the social divisions within the parish, but, with some exceptions, tended to regard the responsibility for reconciliation as the vicar's. Broadly speaking, the parish divided into three areas: the old village; an area of new housing, much of it built by the municipal authorities; and a more developed and prosperous area occupied by business and professional people. Since the building of the mission church to serve the larger part of the second area, the congregation of the parish church tended to think of the parish in terms of the first and third areas only—the old village and the more well-to-do area, or the left and the right-hand sides of the church drive.

To those of the old village—the left-hand side of the drive—the parish had changed a great deal in the last twenty years and mainly for the worse. There was a time when the old village had provided the congregation and officers of the church, when whole streets turned out to church on Sunday, almost to a house, when everyone knew each other and most had been educated together at the church school. Now with declining numbers and an increasing age level amongst the inhabitants of the old village, the centre of the parish had moved to the other side of the church drive. The left-hand side still provided many of the parish workers, and in proportion to their numbers, a generous amount of the finance, but the administration of the parish lay mainly with the right.

> *Business man in 30's:* 'Yes, as far as it goes, I do feel at home in the church, but there has been a loss in personal contact in the parish. It isn't as much of a family as it was twenty years ago. It used to be the same as a country parish where you know everyone and the vicar shares in the concern of the family.'

A. THE CONGREGATION AS A FAMILY

In the three sections of the parish, what was 'done' or 'not done' varied very considerably as far as the rules of friendship and neighbourliness were concerned. In the old village people knew each other, visited each other freely, were frankly interested in other people and their welfare. Members of the congregation in the area tended to have this same friendliness of approach. In the housing estate served by the mission church, people did not know each other nor apparently did they wish to do so. They had been moved into this district from condemned housing in the city. After an initial period of unrest when they had wished to return to 'the other end', the great majority settled down, but they settled into a pattern of life independent of their fellows. It was not uncommon for neighbours of as much as twenty years' standing not to know each other's names, nor to have entered each other's homes. The congregation of the mission church had very largely triumphed over this atmosphere and developed a strong feeling of family concern.

In the third area, more respectable and prosperous than the other two, a different set of rules governing human relationships applied. While a greater degree of initial friendliness was allowable than would be found in the housing estate, definite limits of a fairly arbitrary nature seemed to apply.

> *Housewife in 30's:* 'You may be friendly with people but it doesn't go further than that. It's a question of what is done and what is not done.'

Very generally speaking, the change which had moved the centre of the parish to the right-hand side of the church drive had also resulted in a change in the values governing human relationships. This had many consequences for the development of the congregation as a family.

First, a third of the congregation did not feel a part of a 'family

of worshippers' and a proportion of the remainder limited their
feeling of 'familiness' to their circle of friends and acquaintances.

Housewife in 40's: 'Six people have spoken to me in twenty-one
years.'
Housewife in 50's: 'You see the same people week in week out at
church, but you don't know or speak to them.'
Housewife in 50's: 'I feel that the majority of the congregation want
to go to church and be left alone. If it wasn't for friends in the
Mothers' Union I'd go to church and come home again without
ever speaking to anyone. I had to work my way in.'
Shorthand-typist in 20's: 'The church is supposed to bring you
together. I don't think it does. If you didn't already know someone
—you'd never get to know people just by going to church.'

Only nine members of the sample had asked others of the
congregation to pray for them in times of sickness or trouble.
Half of the remainder felt free to ask for the prayers of fellow
members should the need arise. Some, however, who felt that one
didn't approach other individuals on such a matter, were willing
to ask the vicar.

Secondly, the change of values governing human relations in
the congregation had largely driven out those on the wrong side
of the drive. It was true that the social changes which were reduc-
ing the population in this part of the parish also played a large part
in the gradually decreasing support from this area. Nevertheless
in many cases people felt unwanted and that other churchpeople
looked down upon them.

Cook in 50's: 'They don't encourage you in their homes.'
Housewife in 40's: 'The atmosphere of the church is chilly—there's
no warmth. They don't welcome strangers. I've never felt as if I
belonged.'
Housewife in 50's: 'I was baptized at St Luke's and went to the
school and Sunday-school. My father was churchwarden and I
grew up at St Luke's. But now I've stopped going because people
seem as though they are too good for me—it shouldn't be like that.
You know it hurts terribly to feel that you're not wanted. It isn't

59

that I want fuss—it isn't that. But a word or a smile, perhaps even be shown a seat—and it ought to be like that, oughtn't it?'
Labourer in 40's: 'I sang in the choir of that church for years as a boy and man—but they don't want you. I got tired of having people look down their noses at me. I'm not going back.'

This discomfort did not only come from a different set of rules governing friendliness. Many of those in the more prosperous part of the parish were more conscious of an intellectual difference.

Housewife in 40's: 'We just use the church for the worship of God. We have no common ground with the non-intellectual part of the parish.'

Thirdly, the social and corporate activities of the church lacked the support of the congregation. The right section of the parish did not wish to mix socially with the left, and the villagers were disinclined to risk what they felt to be the snubs of the more prosperous.

Housewife in 50's: 'The parish is in two parts. I would do anything to help a poor child in my work—but socially I don't want to mix with the folk in the other part of the parish—we simply would have nothing in common. I don't think that is snobbish. I don't want to mix with the other part of the parish at church gatherings. We did go once on a parish trip to Lichfield Cathedral—we wanted to see the Cathedral. It's all right if you can go with a group of friends.'

The attempts made to try and bridge the gap by means of social functions had met with disheartening results. In practice, social get-together functions could be as exclusive as they were intended to be inclusive. Not infrequently parishioners left such gatherings more than ever convinced that they were not wanted.

Fourthly, communication regarding the needs of the parish and people tended to break down, both within the Parochial Church Council and outside it. If one section predominated in the Council, the other area felt that there was little point in belonging.

This situation did not apply to the mission church. There the congregation was drawn almost entirely from one locality and felt that they were all 'working-class' people. Curiously enough, the very united nature of the congregation apparently discouraged some from attending. There were some who felt that those who went to the church were 'not their kind'.

It should not be thought that St Luke's was a particularly unfriendly parish. There was indeed no evidence to suggest that it was less friendly than most other Anglican churches in the city.

Housewife in 40's: 'We've moved around a lot and have had our best experience at St Luke's.'

B. THE RELIGIOUS AMENITIES OF THE PARISH

More than three-quarters of the sample felt quite satisfied with the various parish activities as far as their religious needs were concerned. All those who were definitely dissatisfied were women. Amongst the inadequacies mentioned were the lack of individual assistance, the lack of discussion and study groups and the lack of friendliness. Other criticisms included the inadequacy of the Sunday-school which finished at eleven years of age and the hope on the part of one section that Matins might replace Choral Eucharist at 11.0 a.m. on one Sunday in the month. At the mission church, the congregation was unanimous in the need for a resident clergyman.

More than three-quarters of the sample had received a visit from the vicar and a quarter of them had received a visit during the previous six months. The visits of the curate were supplementary to this. While many understood the plight of the vicar attempting to cope with large numbers of people and many calls outside the congregation, the lack of personal contact remained an acutely felt need.

HOW THE CONGREGATION SAW THE WORK OF THE VICAR

To three-quarters of the sample, the role of vicar was ideally one in which the chief quality was sympathetic understanding of the problems of his fellow-men. Seventy-four selected the man of great human understanding, six the brilliant organizer, seven the outstanding preacher, and seven the man of great sanctity.

The work of the vicar was seen as hard, disheartening and under-paid and his success dependent on whether or not nature had endowed him with the 'right' personality. Three functions of the vicar were prominent in people's minds. First, maintaining the services; second, visiting the sick, the congregation and the parish in general; third, the supervising of church organizations, especially those devoted to youth, and building up the congregation as a family.

Some members of the congregation had a more detailed knowledge of the work of the vicar—especially if they were involved in the administration of the parish.

> *Professional man in 40's:* 'Services according to the prayer book; administration of the sacraments; maintenance of the fabric of the church and vicarage buildings; responsibility through the P.C.C. for parish finance; teaching—perhaps in the day-school; visiting the sick, etc.; preparation of candidates for confirmation; marriage guidance; hearing of confessions.'

Again the office of priest, as in St Matthew's, carried little spiritual authority as distinct from any respect earned by the clergyman. Sixteen members of the sample asserted that there were no occasions on which they would call in the parish priest and the response of some of the remainder was not always unqualified. In general the position was much the same as in the parish of St Matthew. Sixty-seven members were prepared to call him in in cases of serious illness or death; 28 for guidance in moral and spiritual problems; and 28 for domestic and other problems.

HOW MEMBERS OF THE CONGREGATION SAW THEIR ROLE IN THE PARISH

To all but a minority, the church was an important institution, but not one which placed them under any kind of obligation. Rather more than half of the sample expressed the belief that there were rules that the Church of England expected its members to observe. These rules chiefly related to the reception of the sacraments, particularly Holy Communion, and the remainder were divided between rules of ethical conduct and what might be termed the etiquette of religious observance.

There was no suggestion that Christianity implied the existence of a fellowship which carried both privileges and obligations. It was felt that the obligations of religion were successfully met by attending church and leading decent lives. No responsibility was felt for the welfare of other church members—if anyone was responsible, it was the vicar. Thus people who could no longer attend church owing to illness, old age, personal or domestic troubles, simply dropped out of the congregation and nothing further was done about them, except perhaps by the vicar. This state of affairs did not exist in the mission church, however, where the troubles of one were the concern of all.

Housewife in 40's: 'My mother-in-law always gave to everything—she's one of the oldest parishioners. No one has called on her from the church for eighteen months—or even inquired. It's made her a bit bitter.'

Widow in 60's: 'I went to church for four years before anyone spoke to me. I lost my husband two and a half years ago and no one has inquired as to how I'm getting on.'

Shopkeeper in 50's: 'When I was ill no one came in to inquire how I was. People come around from the church when they want something. I know we ought to give to the church and I do my best, but I wish the church didn't take an interest in you only when they want something.'

Retired teacher in 70's: 'If you are unable to do very much work for the church I do feel you are in disfavour. No one has time to worry about the older people. When I was ill only one person from the congregation visited me, no one offered to assist with any of the chores. The people who did assist were not churchgoers.'

A quarter of the sample indicated that there was no reason why they shouldn't undertake some work for the church or do more than they were already doing. Explanations of why they were not assisting as much as they could included the unfriendliness of the congregation, never having been asked, the lack of a ready-made opportunity to do the kind of thing they were particularly interested in doing, and not knowing what to do.

> *Works foreman in 40's:* 'Christianity has no meaning in a factory. We are told we must be evangelists and in the back of your mind you must agree—but there is nothing you can do about it.'

HOW MEMBERS OF THE CONGREGATION SAW THEIR POSITION IN A SECULAR WORLD

There was apparently little awareness amongst the sample of any difference in values and behaviour between those inside and those outside the Church. A quarter of the sample did consider that their religious beliefs marked them off—at least on occasions —from those who didn't share them.

A quarter of the sample again were aware of pressures which made it more difficult to live the kind of Christian life they would like to live. These pressures included the general rush of life, circumstances which had left people frustrated and unhappy, and especially the attitude of other people.

> *Housewife in 50's:* 'The neighbours say—Oh, she goes to church— she's a goody goody.'

Two-thirds of the sample could not recall that the behaviour that they expected of themselves as Christians had ever clashed with the expectations of their friends and acquaintances. Not unnaturally, men tended to be aware of this type of situation to a greater extent than women, and factory workers seemed much more conscious of the difficulties than others. People were for the most part convinced that if they were ever faced with a conflict between principle and loyalty to their friends or associates, they would support their principles. A few of the staunchest members, however, who had actually met such situations had no hesitation in admitting that they had chosen loyalty to their group on every occasion.

CHAPTER SIX

ST JOHN'S PARISH

St John's is a large parish in the outer ring of the city. The parish is still largely open farm land, but in the area nearest the city, adjacent to the parish of St Luke's, there is a large housing estate of some 20,000 people. Building is continuing rapidly and one clergyman assisted by a parish worker do what they can to cope with the situation.

The parish was formed in 1934 in response to a need created by the erection of a new housing estate. The estate was well planned, the residential area ranging around the square with its business and shopping centre. The intention of the city authorities in developing this area was to house people from the decaying central portions of the city, and originally a large number of people were poured into the area more or less *en masse*. After a period of initial unsettlement, the people on the estate have become used to their new surroundings. It is, however, generally agreed that the district is devoid of any sort of community feeling.

With the exception of a small area of privately owned houses, the people of the parish are all tenants of the municipal authorities, and most of them work in factories in the outer ring or beyond the city boundaries. The parish is more homogeneous than any of the preceding three.

THE CHURCH

On the outskirts of the estate is the parish church. As there is nothing to take people so far away from the hub of the area, most parishioners are still unaware of the church's existence. The building itself is incomplete and lacks many of the conventional features, such as a tower or bell, that are commonly associated with church architecture. Theoretically the principal Sunday service is the Parish Communion at 9.30 a.m., but Evensong is in fact better attended. In addition to the special services associated with the seasons of the Church, Holy Communion is celebrated daily.

The churchmanship of the members of the congregation is extraordinarily mixed, ranging in background from Irish Protestantism to Anglo-Catholicism. The standard of churchmanship set by St John's itself is a compromise between these two extremes; although less elaborate than St Luke's, it can also be described as 'medium-high'.

The church has had a chequered career. After an encouraging start there were four clergy in twenty years and one year without a vicar at all. The present incumbent had to start building his congregation, handicapped by the resentments of past parochial battles and the shortcomings of two of his predecessors.

The church possesses the usual organizations such as choir, Sunday-school, youth club, Scouts, Brownies, etc., to all of which membership is 'open'.

THE CONGREGATION

Table IV describes the make-up of the congregation in terms of age, sex and marital status.

TABLE IV. COMPOSITION OF THE CONGREGATION

WOMEN

Age	Number	Married	Marital Status Single or widowed
70 plus	–	–	–
60–69	6	4	2
50–59	17	14	3
40–49	16	14	2
30–39	7	6	1
18–29	10	6	4
Total	56	44	12

	MEN		
70 plus	I	I	–
60–69	5	5	–
50–59	8	8	–
40–49	4	4	–
30–39	4	4	–
18–29	5	2	3
Total	27	24	3

The congregation revealed certain striking features: (a) its youth; (b) the overwhelming preponderance of married people; (c) the high proportion of women; and (d) the weakness of the thirty to thirty-nine year age group.

FIGURE X ST JOHN'S PARISH: OCCUPATIONAL STATUS

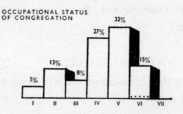

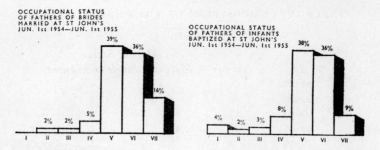

Figure X indicates: (a) the occupational status of the congregation; (b) the occupational status of the fathers of infants baptized at the church during the twelve months prior to the investigation;

(c) the occupational status of the fathers of brides married at the church during the two years previous to the study. The dotted section of the figure indicates the proportion of the congregation non-resident in the parish. As in the previous parishes, the congregation did not appear to be representative of that section of the parish which would normally make use of the occasional offices of the church. The occupational status of the congregation was in general considerably higher.

Only one member of the congregation lived outside the parish. Quite a number of church people in the parish, however, attended other churches on the basis that it didn't matter which church one worshipped at provided one did go to church, so one might just as well go to the church where the building had atmosphere or where the music was better. The parish was also remarkable for another feature—the large number of Anglicans who had taken a keenly active part in the life of the Church for the first twenty, thirty or even fifty years of their lives, still retained their concern for the welfare of the Church, but now had almost or entirely ceased to have any connection with the Church at all. For the most part these people did not fall within the definition of the St John's congregation. The disputes and general instability characteristic of a new parish devoid of a developed tradition, and the upheaval of loyalties which had never previously been detached from the city church at which they had worshipped for so long, seemed to be the most important factors in producing this phenomenon.

> *Foreman in 40's:* 'I used to love going to church. Now at St John's I don't feel any better for going, I don't know quite why. St John's has no atmosphere, it isn't like the old church—you can't feel that you're in God's house.'

The most outstanding factor in the lives of the congregation living on the estate was the long working hours. Men worked six and seven days a week at the factory, leaving early in the morning and not arriving home until late at night. Apart from housewives with young families, the womenfolk were usually out at work, as well as running a home. Household chores had often to be left until the week-end. Home life was still further complicated by the irregular hours resulting from shift work. The police officer who had never yet been home to see his daughter open her presents on Christmas morning and the railway worker who in the first seventeen years of his married life did not have one Sunday off and only one Christmas, typified the general subordination of human interests to the demands of this working environment.

The members of the congregation had a substantial religious background. All but two members felt that religion had been a very marked or a moderate influence in their upbringing. A third of the congregation had at some time in their lives lapsed from active membership in the Church of England, or much more frequently had been members of other denominations. The reasons given by the former group included war experience, long working hours, the care of children and adolescent rebellion. The changes of denomination had chiefly taken place either in youth or at marriage. The woman who was a Baptist until fourteen, became an Anglican, married a Roman Catholic and sent her children to an Elim Sunday-school, indicated the confusing consequences of a complex and disorganized society.

THE RELIGIOUS PRACTICES OF THE CONGREGATION

Figure XI describes the frequency with which the practices of churchgoing, prayer and Bible reading were observed and the frequency with which religious topics were discussed. The practice of churchgoing had in general disintegrated. The modal practice was once a week, but considerably more than half the congregation went less frequently. The infrequency of Bible reading also suggested the disintegration of religious habits.

THE RELIGIOUS BELIEFS OF THE CONGREGATION

Figure XII indicates the degree of belief in the four chosen points of doctrine. There was still a high degree of conformity in belief regarding these points, although the scatter was a great deal more marked than in the other parishes. As before, the greatest divergence was found with regard to the first and last statements and among the younger age groups.

Again, science provided no obstacle to religious belief. In the

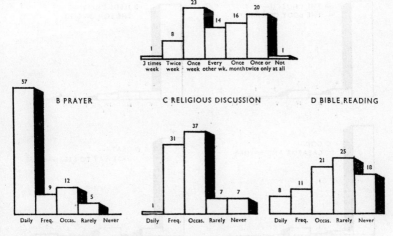

FIGURE XI ST JOHN'S PARISH: RELIGIOUS PRACTICES

A CHURCHGOING

case of the great majority, it was science and not religion that was on trial.

Professional engineer in 30's: 'The findings of science are likely to mess up the earth. The atomic experiments are all wrong.'
Factory worker in 40's: 'The atomic bomb is wicked. The scientists ought to be exterminated—they're a menace.'
Shopkeeper in 60's: 'Scientists have been given the power to find out new inventions and it's up to individuals to use them for good or evil. Now they are being put to wrong uses and are being used mainly for destruction. It's a pity that the Church can't do something about it. I think the Church ought to come forward and give a lead.'

HOW THE CONGREGATION SAW THE PARISH

The general impression of the church members who had

watched the fortunes of the parish fluctuate with the various incumbents, was that at long last the congregation was showing signs of picking up; the present vicar was young and scholarly and his family an asset. Nevertheless the small attendances at the regular services other than major festivals were a source of great concern.

FIGURE XII ST JOHN'S PARISH:RELIGIOUS BELIEFS

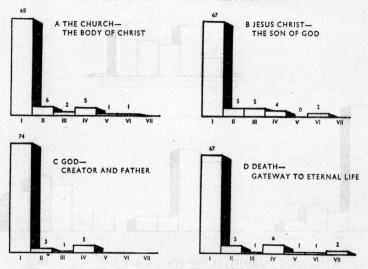

[*The numbers I-VII express the range from untroubled conviction to untroubled doubt: see Questionnaire, pp. 102 f.*]

Widow in 50's: 'It makes me feel sick sometimes to go to the church and see the five or six people there—in an estate of this size it is a shame.'

The one social division of the parish loomed large in the minds of the congregation—the estate and the Park areas. The latter area consisted of the privately owned houses of white-collar workers, usually of managerial or senior status, in contrast to the estate where almost everyone was employed in one capacity or another by industrial plants. There was little social contact between the two areas and each was inclined to suspect that the other received favoured treatment at their own expense.

> *Widow in 50's:* 'All the vicars have always spent most of their time in the Park area—visiting should be the same for everyone, rich or poor.'
> *Housewife in 50's:* 'Visiting is done on the estate but not in the Park area—this is felt by the Park people.'

With so little contact between the two areas it was not surprising that the working position of those on the estate was not always understood.

> *Electrical engineer in 50's:* 'Bed and work make up 95% of the working day, and despite this, the average skilled working man is not getting a living wage. When they get home they're too tired even to visit their friends.'
> *Housewife in 50's:* (Park)—'People seem to live for the factories. I know people have to work, but they even work on Sundays. They seem to live for the factories.'
> *Foreman in 50's:* 'We've been working late and week-ends now for over six months. There's a big boom on at present—I don't know how long it is going to go on. Of course you probably could refuse to do so much overtime, but the boom isn't going to last for ever, and if you did—well you'd be among the first to be put off.'

The church building was generally felt to lack the atmosphere of the old-established parish church with its traditional architecture and stained glass windows. These things did matter. Brides had even preferred to be married in other churches rather than have to sign the register in a church where there was no vestry. The differing backgrounds of the congregation made it difficult to provide services to satisfy all tastes.

> *Housewife in 40's:* 'More often now we go to a lower church not too far away. St John's is not very high, I know, but the high church trimmings annoy me—you must feel at home in the church you go to.'

73

Housewife in 30's: 'The services are not sufficiently Catholic. I go as a duty and in the desire (rather selfishly) to try to get comfort from the Communion service and the peace it always offers.'

Housewife in 30's: 'The 11.30 service on the radio on Sunday morning is so simple and homely—I wish it could be like that in church. On the radio the sermons are homely, it could be you that was being talked about; but in church I get lost at the beginning of the service and never find anything to grip on to.'

A. THE CONGREGATION AS A FAMILY

The lack of a family atmosphere was more strongly felt in St John's than in the other parishes. Only 18 members of the congregation felt part of a 'family of worshippers', 48 definitely not, and 17 were doubtful. This feeling was not linked to any particular group. The general characteristic of the parish was one of anonymity.

Housewife in 50's: 'It's not homely, there's no friendliness. I don't think they (the congregation) visit one another even though they are such a handful.'

Single woman in 60's: 'We meet people at church, then we go our several ways home and we don't see them until next week.'

Housewife in 20's: 'I've only been here about five years and am just beginning to know people.'

Housewife in 40's: 'I've been attending regularly for ten years and still don't know anyone.'

While most members merely felt that they didn't know each other, there were those who felt definitely unwanted or uncomfortable.

Housewife in 40's: 'The others used to go three times a Sunday, now they only go once. I go occasionally, but none of us feel wanted. We feel that they look down on us.'

Housewife in 40's: 'The other people are very much better off than we are and I feel a bit uncomfortable at church. I've had to put off buying new clothes because we've got to save enough to take the family to the seaside for a week, and the others must feel I'm a bit of a drab.'

Despite all the handicaps to the development of the family life of the church, there was nothing that made it impossible.

> *Housekeeper in 40's:* 'I feel in St John's as I've never felt in another church. I feel that it is my church. It may be poor but it is my parish church and I feel at home and have made many friends there.'

B. THE RELIGIOUS AMENITIES OF THE PARISH

Three-quarters of the congregation were satisfied with the various parish activities as meeting their religious needs. Among the reasons given for dissatisfaction were the lack of friendliness, discussion groups for youth, social gatherings for young wives and mothers, and the lack of Matins. Matins was frequently preferred for its own sake as a service, as being more suitable for children, and also for working people whose only chance of sleeping in was Sunday morning.

> *Factory worker in 40's:* '9.30 is too early for working people. Sunday morning is the only chance to sleep in a bit and you can still get to church if it is at 11.0.'
>
> *Housewife in 30's:* 'If you go to the 8.0 a.m. service, you can't get back in time to take the children at 9.30. It isn't a suitable service for children anyway.'
>
> *Retired woman in 60's:* 'I do like Matins myself and there's a lot of praise in it—the *Te Deum* is lovely. Matins once a month would be a help.'

All but 15 members of the congregation had been visited by the vicar, and half of these had received at least one visit in the previous six months. This was additional to the regular visiting of the parish worker. The difficulty of visiting in a parish of such a size was appreciated, especially as people were away from home so much, but the lack of personal contact which visiting could give, was greatly felt.

HOW THE MEMBERS OF THE CONGREGATION SAW THE WORK OF THE VICAR

The role of vicar was felt ideally to be that of a 'universal friend'. Sixty-two seized upon great human understanding as the quality most to be desired in their vicar; 15 selected the outstanding preacher; five the brilliant organizer; and one only the man of great sanctity.

The work of the vicar was seen as hard and disheartening. The specific nature of his duties was often far from clear, but two functions were of great importance. First, was getting to know people by visiting the congregation and as far as possible the parish as a whole—personal contact was the essence of his job. Second, was the conduct of the various services and the supervision of the church organizations.

Eleven members of the congregation asserted that there were no circumstances in which they would call in the parish priest, and a further nine declared that it depended entirely upon his character.

> *Carpenter in 40's:* 'I'm rather doubtful whether there are any circumstances. I am a great believer in myself and I believe in believing in myself.'
> *Business manager in 50's:* 'A true Christian shouldn't need the parish priest.'

Sixty-nine members were inclined to call in the vicar in cases of serious illness or death, 33 for domestic or other problems, and 27 for guidance in moral or spiritual questions.

HOW THE MEMBERS OF THE CONGREGATION SAW THEIR ROLE IN THE PARISH

The Church was not seen as an institution which laid obligations upon its members—it existed to provide services. Slightly more than half the congregation declared themselves unaware of any rules which, as members of the Church of England, they were expected to observe. Rules most often suggested were related to the use of the sacraments and attendance at Holy Communion.

The church was not seen as a fellowship, nor was fellowship regarded as integral to the process of worship. Only 18 members of the congregation had asked others to pray for them or their families. Approximately half of the remainder felt free to do so if the occasion arose. Such a practice was not always regarded as desirable. Religion was a personal matter between oneself and the Deity and had nothing to do with other people.

> *Professional engineer in 30's:* 'No—I wouldn't dream of it. You've got to have faith for yourself, it's no good asking others.'

There was, as in the other parishes, a large untapped reserve of willingness to assist in the work of the parish. Almost one-third of the congregation felt that they could be doing more to assist, and explained their inactivity with reference to past parochial disputes; the lack of family atmosphere; the presence of the cliques; and a desire not to offend people responsible for certain specific tasks.

> *Housewife in 40's:* 'I'd love to do little things, but you have to push so hard. If I was asked I should be pleased but I wouldn't push myself. There's a group there, and you feel you're not wanted. The clique looks down on you.'

HOW THE MEMBERS OF THE CONGREGATION SAW THEIR POSITION IN A SECULAR WORLD

Almost one-third of the congregation was conscious of occasions when their religious beliefs marked them off from those who didn't share them; of pressures which made it difficult to live the Christian life they would like, and of occasions when the behaviour they expected of themselves as Christians clashed with the expectations of their friends and associates. The situations for the most part arose out of the attitude of non-churchgoers and the pressure and conditions of work.

The clash between the expectations of churchgoers and the

expectations of their friends and associates was found to have developed a curious twist. The following examples testify to the confused state of the general religious environment.

> *Housewife in 30's:* 'After we've all been to church on Sunday morning, my son sometimes goes out in the afternoon and plays football. My relatives, who never go to church, are horrified that he is allowed to do such things on a Sunday.'
>
> *Housewife in 20's:* 'Sometimes I've had to do some washing on a Sunday and I've felt quite uneasy about it because I felt that one set of our neighbours wouldn't approve, but they are not people who ever go to church.'

Again, people generally found difficulty in deciding whether or not to continue the practices of saying grace, kneeling for prayers and maintaining Lenten discipline in the presence of people who might perhaps have no sympathy with religious observance.

CHAPTER SEVEN

THE SOCIAL CONTEXT OF THE CONGREGATION

THE Church of England is essentially a parochial institution; its whole range of activities is built upon the foundation of its parish life. Like all social institutions, the Church does not exist in a vacuum but is involved in larger social situations. The life of the parishes studied was determined to a very large degree by their existence in a metropolitan city dedicated to the furtherance of industry.

The most important characteristic of such a city, humanly speaking, is the lack of any sense of community; the widespread decline in what sociologists have called 'primary group' relationships in terms of locality or neighbourhood, and, as a result of the substitution of contiguity for community, an expansion in the range of associations only on the impersonal secondary level. In a city the size of Birmingham, it is increasingly difficult to find fragments of neighbourhood where groups of families really know each other personally, visit and assist each other and are engaged in the mutual exchange of goods and services. The sense of neighbourhood is constantly threatened by the mobility of the population, the invasion of residential areas by business concerns and the dispersion of friends and the centres of working, shopping, leisure time and even religious activities.

The city dweller lives constantly among a mass of people, and is dependent upon the specialized services which they can offer. But he has no personal relationship with them. The individual urbanite acquires membership in a wide variety of groups, each of which functions with regard to one aspect of his personality. Individuals come to exist as anonymous fragments which come to life only with regard to their specific roles in a series of independent groups. As a result, social experience becomes fractional and 'the total personality is less known to any group and has less opportunity for expression'.[1]

Certain findings are relevant at this point:

(i) The considerable divergence between the occupational status of the congregation and that of the parishioners who used the church for marriages and baptisms.

(ii) The varying composition of the four congregations in accordance with the social circumstances of the parish.

(iii) The varying proportion of each congregation resident in its parish as determined by the position of the parish in the city.

The following conclusions are suggested:

The parishes are no longer meaningful social or neighbourhood units.
In a mainly rural England the parish was a natural community. Urban life has altered the situation and the four parishes, with the possible exception of St John's, are now little more than ecclesiastical administrative areas. Nor are the parish churches the centre of social life as they had been in the past. They are not intimately linked with local groups; they do not express group concern; and they are not instruments of group action.

The parish churches reflect in detail the conditions of life in a large city.
Many of the distinctive features of the four parishes were taken, chameleonlike, from their social surroundings. Locality would suggest that, other factors being equal, the parishes of St Mark's and St Matthew's were declining and St Luke's and St John's were growing. The large proportion of elderly people and single and widowed women in the inner city parishes as contrasted with the more balanced congregation of St Luke's and the youthful married congregation of St John's is the result of urban growth and

[1] E. C. Lindeman, 'Community', *The Encyclopaedia of Social Sciences*, vol. 4 (New York: Macmillan, 1931), p. 105.

brings its own distinctive problems. The increasingly absentee congregation and the declining link with the parish of St Matthew's, the divorce between congregation and parish which is virtually complete in the case of St Mark's, the social tensions of St Luke's and the disintegration of the social and religious life of St John's—all these are typical church problems originating in society at large. It seems entirely reasonable to suppose that these phenomena will be found in every parish similarly placed.

The churches are congregational rather than parochial in character.

In none of the four parishes is the congregation remotely representative of the people of the parish as a whole—not even of those who use the occasional offices of the Church. It seems unlikely that the parish has any influence on the mass of indifferent people within its boundaries. Even amongst churchgoers, friendships, family loyalties, churchmanship, architecture and music are as often the deciding factor in their choice of church as is locality.

If the parochial system is to survive as a living expression of the social structure of English life, parishes must not only reorganize themselves, if necessary, but also attempt to create a sense of community at levels below that of worship.

If the church is to convert the parish into a worshipping community, it would seem necessary first to create a community in which social consciousness can grow through deepening the significance of mutual relationships. The attempt to re-establish group life in the midst of the anonymous secondary relationships of the city would appear to justify some attempt on the part of the churches not only to provide for the spiritual needs of their people, but also to provide a social centre and an education integrated with moral and spiritual values.

CHAPTER EIGHT

THE FELLOWSHIP OF THE CONGREGATION

THE congregations were not fellowships with a specifically Anglican ideology which united them and distinguished them from other secular and religious groups. With the exception of the nuclear members of each congregation, they were collections of individuals who met together to worship as they would meet on other social occasions. The relationships within the churches had the same impersonal quality as the secondary group relationships of other social organizations.

With the fragmentation of social life the church had now only a limited claim upon the interests of church members, for they were also members of other groups, political parties, lodges, clubs, etc., so that a person could no longer be identified solely in terms of his religion. His membership in the religious group was only one of his several specialized interests and a minor part of his total experience. Indeed, religious membership rarely appeared to have an integrating function. Relatively few church members were on mutual visiting terms with other members, yet not infrequently, one found that members who had visited each other had done so, not because of mutual church membership but because of their membership in a political party or some other organization. The political party had succeeded where the church had failed.

A considerable amount of evidence related to this problem.

(i) A large number of people felt unwanted and out of place even though in many cases they were regular churchgoers. This was more common among women than men who depended less upon the church for their social relationships. The feeling was least in the small homogeneous mission church to St Luke's and greatest in the case of St John's.

(ii) The Church was not seen as a fellowship by the majority of members, nor as involving obligations.

(iii) In the parishes of St Matthew's, St Luke's and St John's, those who were handicapped by ill-health or old age, or were limited in their movement by young families, frequently dropped out of the congregation. Vicars themselves might or might not visit, but whole families in such circumstances felt deserted by their group.

(iv) The congregations reflected rather than reconciled social divisions.

(v) There was a breakdown of communication between the different sections of the congregations.

(vi) Enormous appeal was exerted by the quality of 'great human understanding' in a vicar.

(vii) There were innumerable complaints that the churches were unfriendly, that they were not like country churches, that the vicars were unknown to them, that the people never spoke to them, that the church did not seem interested in them, etc.

(viii) The overwhelming majority of people were unaware of any actual tension between the values of the Church and the values of society.

(ix) There was a tendency to avoid situations in which tensions might arise. Under certain circumstances or on principle, religion was avoided as a topic of conversation and distinctive practices had very largely been given up.

The following conclusions are suggested:

The parish church is unable to provide the necessary environment as a nursery of sanctity in which the individual can stabilize his belief against the fluctuations of circumstances, the weaker members receive support and encouragement and the more vigorous, discipline and guidance.

As the congregations were not fellowships, there was no body on to which to graft new members. It was significant that marriage provided the chief means of recruitment of new adult members of the church—a person could become attached to another individual even if there was no fellowship to join.

Quite naturally, the Church as an organized society includes people in various stages of growth and even the best are imperfect. It cannot be expected that they will all manifest 'the fruits of the Spirit' in equal degree. Inevitably the Church could be expected to encourage the development within the congregation of small groups which would realize among themselves the relations of mutual trust, support and responsibility characteristic of Christian society. These groups would be expected to widen their borders until the congregation really did become a fellowship.

The values of church members are for the most part drawn from the other secular groups in which they have membership. In general this means that the ways of correct behaviour and values are one or other of the species of middle-class values, exalted by their association with the Church.

However sound and responsible these values might be in some respects, they had inevitable limitations. Moral values ceased to have any apparent link with the Christian revelation—they were after all drawn from a social and not a supernatural context. The limitations were most apparent at a simple level. One didn't go round talking about religion, one didn't ask for the prayers of other people, and one didn't get into casual conversation with people one met, even if the meeting-place were the church. In the sense that the Gospel had failed to revolutionize the lives of church members, it would be true to say that much churchgoing was conventional. Exhortations to behave in ways unnatural in social life met with no response. Claims and practices distinctive to the Church were abandoned. Only when church members were freed from the prevailing customs by especial circumstances or by the forging of a real fellowship in which customs appropriate to the needs of the Church could be realized, could such handicapping restrictions be overcome.

The appeal of the Church rests on social compatibility rather than doctrinal conviction.

As a result of the lack of a distinctive ideology and a fellowship which overrode other considerations, the life of the parish church tended to reflect the divisions of society rather than reconcile and heal them. The church not unnaturally tended to take on the class character of its locality and become identified with the kind of people who were near it. Where the neighbourhood consisted of more than one type of social group, the predominant group tended to displace the others. Even St Mark's, which had held an almost entirely absentee congregation together by the strength of its doctrinal convictions and was the only group to include all seven occupational status ratings, had gradually acquired a social distinction between those living inside and those living outside the parish. This might well have barred parishioners from their own church, had not the newcomers been largely Roman Catholic or Muslim.

Members representing all the social classes and all grades of occupational strata were to be found within the four congregations —in itself this might well be a unique achievement amongst voluntary social organizations, even if the proportions were heavily weighted towards the more 'well-to-do'. The distribution of such people, was, however, far from indiscriminate.

The mission church to St Luke's was largely made up of people who regarded themselves as 'working class'; a most friendly and united church. There was some evidence to suggest that other people in the area who felt that they ranked somewhat higher in the social scale, declined to attend where the congregation was not made up of 'our kind of people'. St Matthew's staunchly continued to make its appeal to the kind of people who originally lived in the area, despite their continued exodus from the centre of the city. St Luke's revealed the almost complete triumph of the newer suburb dwellers over those of the old village. In St John's the distinction between the estate and the Park dwellers had not yet resulted in a conclusive decision for either party. Victory must almost inevitably lie with the overwhelming numerical superiority of the estate and already there was a strong tendency for Park dwellers to attend other parish churches.

Instead of the parish church's revealing a fellowship which manifested a new system of right relationships, testified to the reality of the Gospel and drew people to it by the evidence of a new quality of life not to be found elsewhere, it was in fact cut off from a very large section of its people by its social allegiance and assumptions. It offered the Gospel on impossible terms—endangering their acceptance in groups where the Church had no place, offering membership in a group which was alien, suspicious and unlikely to accept those who were clearly not the 'right' people.

The Church is powerless to influence its environment or to judge, redeem and transform social facts and movements, despite its claim to a unique revelation of the nature and destiny of man.

The lack of a distinctive Christian fellowship paralyses the action of the Church upon society in two ways. Firstly, the current values of Birmingham society are not seen by the great majority of churchpeople as alien to those of the Church, or at least as an obstacle to the Christian faith. In consequence, the Church is too enmeshed in its social context to be able to pass judgment on it; it has nothing distinctive to offer.

Secondly, the indirect influence of the Church on society is dependent upon the very nature of its fellowship, upon its simply being—the Church. 'Let the Church be the Church' is a statement the importance of which has not yet been fully realized among churchpeople. The Church is the force which in the name of God, judges, redeems and transforms the world by being itself a universal fellowship in Christ in which there is neither Jew nor Gentile, working class nor middle class, 'right' nor 'wrong' people. Without a fellowship, the Church is deprived of the means by which it influences society either directly or indirectly.

CHAPTER NINE

THE CLIMATE OF OPINION IN THE CONGREGATION

THE CONCEPT OF THE CHURCH

IN the minds of the members of the congregations there was no clear conception of the Church, its nature and purpose.

The Church was felt to be either:

(i) a kind of club brought into existence by churchgoing; an agency for the teaching of sound morals;

or (ii) a visible divine society, the 'body of Christ', calling its members not to mere 'goodness', but to share mystically in the life of the risen, ascended, glorified Christ, a fellowship designed to leaven and redeem the world, to win all men to Christ by witnessing to his resurrection and to proclaim in its own fellowship the liberating and revolutionary powers of the Gospel.

The general pattern of opinion in St Matthew's, St Luke's and St John's held to the first of these views. The working nucleus of the congregation in these parishes however to some extent provided an exception. The prevailing attitude in St Mark's favoured the second view as a result of its more direct links with the Oxford Movement.

On the basis of this the following conclusions are suggested:

Where the Church has not made clear the obligations of membership, they are taken from the prevailing social code of the groups from which members are drawn.

The Anglican Church has placed enormous emphasis on spiritual freedom and has preferred to place reliance on pastoral guidance rather than dictate how any soul may best receive the fullness of

God's help through the operation of a set of rules. Owing to the chaotic state of Canon Law it is not altogether clear whether the Anglican Church has any rules or, if it has, precisely what they are. It is generally accepted that the only requirement for laity insisted upon by the Prayer Book is that they attend Holy Communion three times a year of which Easter must be one.

The investigation revealed certain factors:

(i) St Mark's was the congregation in which it was made clear that membership involved definite obligations other than the rule above. Members might not fulfil their obligations but they were aware that they were wrong not to have done so. This congregation also revealed the greatest development of religious practices amongst individuals beyond the minimum requirements; the closest understanding between vicar and people; and the greatest amount of personal attention through confession and visiting.

(ii) The great majority of church members were unaware of the minimum requirement regarding Communion.

(iii) Members often cited rules which were not in fact authoritative.

(iv) Where members were unaware of the Church's conception of itself and the obligations due to it, it did not necessarily follow that they had no implicit idea of the Church, its nature and obligations. Where the emphasis was on good works, responsible parenthood, and sound citizenship, the concept of the Church and its duties was that prevailing in the social group.

(v) Whether people operated on the minimum requirement of the Church or the norms of the social group, their observance was equally open to fulfilment, and the error of complacency.

The maintenance of the Church as an institution tends to become an end in itself.

Because the functions of the Church are seen in social rather than supernatural terms, the chief purposes of the institution tend to be overlooked. Especially did this difficulty arise in a struggling parish, where more and more work came to rest on increasingly few people. Almost all the energies of the congregation were directed into maintenance and little or nothing into pastoral care. Illustrative of this tendency were the emotionally vested interests which centred round certain aspects of church work, the development of cliques, and the assessment of other members in terms of their usefulness in the maintenance of the church. Hence the undue attention to the young and vigorous and the neglect of the sick and elderly.

Sanctity becomes irrelevant.

With individual exceptions, sanctity tended to be an alien ideal in all but St Mark's parish. It did not seem to have any place in the values of the social groups with which members were identified. This could be expected to have a depressing effect on the level of lay religious aspiration. The lack of favour shown for the man of great sanctity as the ideal vicar was very largely due to the belief that he would be unpractical and unable to deal with the business side of the church. In addition, however, there was a positive distrust—even fear—of sanctity as an ideal. This did not preclude a respect for sanctity in the form of 'goodness' when perceived in other people.

Charles Morgan in an essay on 'The Empty Pews' suggested that there was a connection between the increasing concern with administration, central planning and control on the one hand and decreasing congregations on the other. He also claimed that a premium was placed on organizing ability and administration in preference to saintliness, philosophy and scholarship.

> 'The error is the error, which is the curse of modern civilization, of judging men and institutions not by what they are inwardly but by what they do apparently. Priests are promoted because they are active in good works and have the attributes of an efficient civil servant; they are sometimes scorned and passed over as being intellectually aloof if they devote their lives to meditation and the exercises of the spirit.'[1]

[1] Charles Morgan, *Reflections in a Mirror* (London: Macmillan, 1946), p. 149.

Whatever the standards might be by which clergy judged their own success or failure, these standards are those of the bulk of the laity. Only in St Mark's were sanctity and faithfulness to the obligations of office valued more highly.

THE ROLE OF THE CLERGY

Most members of the congregation had no clear idea of the role of the vicar.

The question in which people were asked to imagine that they had become the vicar of the parish and to suggest the tasks which they would be expected to undertake was by far the most difficult. Certain points did emerge from the survey.

(i) The work of the vicar was seen as hard, disheartening and underpaid. Only in St Mark's was his work redeemed by enormous privileges.

(ii) The success or failure of the clergy was largely determined by the standard of enjoyment which the services provided and by the size of the congregation.

(iii) The office of vicar carried little authority, even in the spiritual sphere. To many of the congregation there was little that he could do.

As a result of the findings, three conclusions are put forward: *The position and role of the clergy have become ambiguous and uncertain.*

The functions of the clergy, both social and ecclesiastical, have undergone considerable change during the past century. In the days of a mainly rural England, the clergyman had an assured, central and recognized place in the social structure of the community as well as in the ecclesiastical structure of the Church. During the last seventy-five years the vicar has lost his position in local government, philanthropy and education; and the influence and authority of the pulpit has been reduced by the Press and Radio.

The pastoral role of the clergy has suffered particularly in the parishes where the vicar is now responsible for as many as 20,000 people. There is little he can do in the face of such numbers to get to know people individually and help them in the growth of their spiritual life. There was no common understanding of the task of the clergy amongst three of the four congregations. Hence what was expected of the clergyman differed from person to person. The proverbial tactlessness of the vicar could usually be accounted for as a result of this confusion of roles.

The primary cause of the serious decline in the quantity and quality of the clergy is not so much financial (as is often claimed) but is rather due to the failure of the Church to redefine the tradition and theology of the ministry in terms of the social conditions in which it is to function.[1]

The importance of the clergy's knowing the nature of their duties and the techniques for performing them was stressed as long ago as the seventeenth century, by Richard Baxter, in his classic, *The Reformed Pastor*. More recently the same point has been analysed by Gustafson in an important article. 'The problem the minister faces in any social context,' he asserted, 'is that of determining who he is and what he is doing within the complexity of his functions.'

Too often, he suggested, training for ordination had not given the minister 'on the one hand, a theological doctrine of the ministry and, on the other hand, a sociological definition of his task. If he has worked out either of these, he has frequently not integrated the two so that he can find some basis of legitimation for many of his specific activities within the gospel and tradition of the Church.'[2]

The absence of clarity as to the role of minister has been emphasized in the various solutions put forward to deal with the

[1] (1925) 'The extent of the decline in social importance which has befallen the clergy during the last century is difficult to appreciate and almost impossible to overstate. It has marched with a continual lowering of their intellectual equipment until it would really seem impossible that we can fall lower.' E. F. Braley (ed.), *More Letters of Herbert Hensley Henson* (London: S.P.C.K., 1954), p. 43.

[2] J. M. Gustafson, 'An Analysis of the Problem of the Role of the Ministry', *Journal of Religion*, 34, 1954, p. 187.

serious lack of clergy. Robinson asserted that the theological colleges were 'not turning out *confident* men, not confident in themselves (which God forbid), but confident that they know what is required of them and that they are technically equipped to meet it'.[1] Blair referred to 'the "inferiority complex" about their position which appears to be one of the chief weaknesses of a not inconsiderable number of priests today and one of the chief causes of disagreement and misunderstanding in many parishes'.[2] While some writers and spokesmen of the Church referred to the importance of the ministry as a profession, others stressed the importance of the development of the non-professional ministry. The contemporary inability of the Church of England to make up her mind and state openly what she does understand by the Church's ministry, places a heavy burden of responsibility for the success of the mission of the gospel on the minister's personality.

Nor is the office of priest the only one to be affected by the lack of clarity as to the aim of the Church's ministry in the present social situation. The Archbishops of York and Canterbury in a recent appeal for deaconesses were reported as stating that: 'At her ordination as a deaconess a woman receives by episcopal ordination a distinctive and permanent status' in the Church.[3] What that 'distinctive and permanent status' might be, however, is something on which the Church has so far failed to agree. When a deaconess does manage to carve out for herself a distinctive status and sphere of activity in a diocese, it is almost solely due to her own ability and persistence—the Church cannot take the credit for it.

To suggest that much of the failure of recruiting to the ministry is linked to the lack of clarity as to the role, is not to decry the importance of finance as a factor. It must be conceded at once that clerical stipends have been in general grossly inadequate and

[1] J. A. T. Robinson, 'The Theological College in a Changing World', *Theology*, 55, 1952, p. 207.

[2] A. Blair, 'Ordination Candidates and the War', *Theology*, 46, 1943, p. 173.

[3] *The Birmingham Post*, 5th November 1954.

even today leave much to be desired. When churchpeople, however, described their relief when their son finally decided against being ordained, or asserted that their schoolboy son was not going to enter the ministry if they could help it, they were not thinking of finance.

As the ambiguity is more characteristic of the pastoral than the priestly role, clergy representing the Protestant element of the Anglican tradition will be more seriously affected than those representing the Catholic.

Almost the only aspect of the work of the clergy which has remained unchanged is the priestly function of representing God to man and man to God. The emphasis here is with the regular and continuous acts of worship and communion with God. In the parish of St Mark's there was as a whole a very different set of expectations on the part of the congregation. The Anglo-Catholic conception of the priest was clear and unambiguous.

If these conclusions are valid, it could be expected that 'high-church' dioceses would recruit more and abler clergy than the evangelical. It would be difficult to substantiate this, but it might very well account for the evidence suggesting that not only does the Northern Province with its evangelical dioceses receive a smaller share of the assistant curates than the South, but that it also produces proportionately fewer ordination candidates.[1]

THE ROLE OF THE LAITY

Churchpeople had no clear idea as to their role in the life of the Church.

Certain facts emerged from the survey:

(i) In the minds of churchpeople there was a clear distinction between the function and nature of the clergy and of the laity, alike in the Catholic and the Protestant versions of the Anglican tradition. It is true that few were clear as to what the function of each ought to be, but the distinction was there. The ministry of

[1] Cf. the correspondence in *Theology* from February to April 1949.

the Gospel was a function of the professional ministry, not of the layman.

(ii) Each of the four congregations appeared to have a large reserve of labour which was untapped. The two most common reasons why it remained so were that people didn't know what to do, and the kind of things that people wished to do did not fit into the framework of current parish activity.

(iii) Almost all the activity in the four congregations was purely domestic. The only reaching out into the parishes was through the church schools in the case of St Mark's and St Luke's, through the Sunday-schools and Youth Organizations and through the occasional offices conducted by the vicar.

(iv) There were no adult groups in any of the four churches of either a devotional or study nature. The exception to this was the little mission church to St Luke's.

(v) With the exception of the nucleus of each congregation and to a larger extent the congregation of St Mark's, the church was not seen as a fellowship.

The following three conclusions are suggested:

The lack of clarity in the role of the laity reflects the indecision of the Church.

The reluctance to explore the implications of lay activity was well illustrated in the report of the Commission on Evangelism. 'The inalienable right and duty of the laity to take its full part in the spiritual work of the Church finds forceful expression all down the Church's history.'[1] The problem is not whether the laity has a right to take its 'full part' in the spiritual work of the Church, but what in terms of specific roles and functions does that 'full part' involve? Expressions such as 'the priesthood of the laity' or the right of the laity to the 'priesthood of all believers'[2] are only confusing as long as their implications are not made clear.

Necessity revived the lay office of Reader in the middle of the last century. This recognized form of ministry has been described

[1] *Towards the Conversion of England*, p. 58.   [2] *Ibid.*, p. 61.

as 'the last resort of distracted church-wardens' and as 'an office which the Church in acknowledging so half-heartedly seems almost to despise'.[1] This office is open to men only. Such blanket expressions as 'the priesthood of the laity' are not in themselves a solution to the problems of what can be done and by whom.

The Church is able to inspire its members to work for other philanthropic and social agencies more successfully than for itself.

The number of churchpeople working for various voluntary social and philanthropic organizations was remarkable. Many churchpeople were responding to the message of the Gospel through secular channels. The church itself appeared to offer no openings for its members who responded to its own teaching.

The parish churches are without any form of strategy.

The lack of accepted roles and responsibilities amongst the members made strategy impossible. There was no red-hot centre to the congregation, no study or devotional group for developing a team or teams of 'militants'. The energy of the nucleus was exhausted by church maintenance, and no opportunity was given members to test their faith in action. There were many people who would have agreed that 'England will never be converted until the laity use the opportunities for evangelism daily afforded by their various professions, crafts and occupations',[2] but were unable either to recognize these theoretically numerous opportunities or know what to do about them when they appeared. Until such questions are answered, exhortations to evangelism remain a polite formality to which no one is actually expected to respond.

[1] F. Bennett, 'Money or Men', *Theology*, 50, 1947, p. 51.
[2] *Towards the Conversion of England*, p. 58.

APPENDIX

THE INTERVIEW SCHEDULE

THE INTERVIEW SCHEDULE

1. Do you feel that you need some form of religious belief in order to live a full and happy life?

>   .... Yes
>   .... No
>   .... Doubtful

2. Do you feel as though you are a part of a 'family of worshippers' at St ——?

>   .... Yes
>   .... No
>   .... Doubtful

3. Have you ever asked other members of the congregation to pray for you or your family, when in sickness or trouble?

>   .... Yes
>   .... No
>   .... Doubtful

a) *If no*—Would you feel free to do so if the occasion arose?

>   .... Yes
>   .... No
>   .... Doubtful

4. Do you feel that on the whole, the parish activities of St —— satisfactorily meet your religious needs?

>   .... Yes
>   .... No
>   .... Doubtful

a) *If no*—In what way do the parish activities fail to meet your religious needs?

5. Most social organizations and clubs have some rules which their members have to agree to stand by.
Are you aware of any rules that the Church of England expects its members to observe?

>   .... Yes
>   .... No
>   .... Doubtful

a) *If yes*—What rules does the Church of England expect its members to observe?

6. When a water-pipe bursts you call in the plumber; when you sprain an ankle you send for the doctor—under what circumstances would you call in the parish priest?

7. You have, let us imagine, been recently ordained, and have been appointed vicar of the parish of St —— in the diocese of Birmingham. What duties would you expect to be called upon to undertake in that position?

8. You have been made responsible for selecting a suitable successor for the Rev. ——, who has moved to another part of the diocese. You are given the choice of four men, each of whom is outstanding in one direction; one is a brilliant organizer, another an outstanding preacher, the third has a remarkable gift for human relationships and human understanding, and the fourth is a man of unusual sanctity and devotion. Which of the four would you choose?

>   .... The brilliant organizer
>   .... The outstanding preacher
>   .... The man of great human understanding
>   .... The man of great sanctity

a) What are the reasons which determined your choice?

9. Has the vicar ever visited you?

.... Yes
.... No
.... Doubtful

a) *If yes*—Has the vicar visited you within the last six months?

.... Yes
.... No
.... Doubtful

10. To what degree has religion been an influence in your upbringing?

.... Very marked
.... Moderate
.... Slight
.... None at all

11. Has there been a time in your life when you were not an active member of the Church of England?

.... Yes
.... No
.... Doubtful

a) *If yes*—During which part of your life?

b) *If yes*—How did this come about?

12. Do you feel that you could be serving the Church more fully than you are doing at present?

.... Yes
.... No
.... Doubtful

a) *If yes*—Is there anything in particular you would like to be doing?

b) *If yes*—Is there anything which prevents you from serving the Church as fully as you would like to?

13. Which of the following statements best describes your usual practice?

a) During the past six months you have gone to Church

     .... About twice a week
     .... About once a week
     .... About once every other week
     .... On an average once a month
     .... Once or twice only
     .... Not at all

b) During the past six months you have prayed

     .... Daily
     .... Frequently
     .... Occasionally
     .... Rarely
     .... Never

c) During the past six months you have discussed religious problems with your family or friends

     .... Daily
     .... Frequently
     .... Occasionally
     .... Rarely
     .... Never

d) During the past six months you have read a passage of the Bible or of some devotional book

     .... Daily
     .... Frequently
     .... Occasionally
     .... Rarely
     .... Never

14. Please indicate the number on the scale which best describes the degree of your belief in the following statements.

a) The Church is the 'body of Christ'—the surest foundation of civilized life.

1	2	3	4	5	6	7
I am quite convinced it is true		It may well be true but it does not affect my life			I am quite convinced it is untrue	

b) Jesus Christ is the Son of God and Saviour of men.

1	2	3	4	5	6	7
I am quite convinced it is true		It may well be true but it does not affect my life			I am quite convinced it is untrue	

c) There is one God of infinite power, wisdom and goodness, Creator of the universe, whose relationship with man is a personal one—that of a Father.

1	2	3	4	5	6	7
I am quite convinced it is true		It may well be true but it does not affect my life			I am quite convinced it is untrue	

d) Death is but the gateway to eternal life.

1	2	3	4	5	6	7
I am quite convinced it is true		It may well be true but it does not affect my life			I am quite convinced it is untrue	

15. How do you feel about the often mentioned conflict between the findings of science and the main beliefs of religion?

     .... To my mind religion and science clearly support one another
     .... The conflict is negligible (i.e. more apparent than real)
     .... The conflict is considerable but probably not irreconcilable
     .... The conflict is very considerable, perhaps irreconcilable
     .... The conflict is definitely irreconcilable

16. Do you feel that your religious beliefs in any way mark you off

from other people who don't share them, so that sometimes you feel embarrassed or isolated because of these views?

.... Yes
.... No
.... Doubtful

17. Are you aware of any pressures which tend to make it more difficult for you to live the kind of Christian life you would like to live?

.... Yes
.... No
.... Doubtful

a) *If yes*—What pressures are you aware of?

18. Please describe your reactions to the following situations:
   a) You have a visitor coming to dinner, so far as you know one who has no interest in religion. Normally you say grace before meals. What are you most likely to do on this occasion?
   b) You are walking with a friend. An elderly man stops you and begs for money. What would your reaction be?
   c) You are attending a week-end conference. The members of the conference are on the whole unsympathetic to religion. You are sharing a room with another member whom you have not met before. Normally you would say your evening prayers in a kneeling position. What course of action would you adopt on finding that you were both preparing to retire for the night at the same time?
   d) As part of your Lenten discipline you have given up cakes and biscuits. You are visiting some people you do not know very well and your hostess makes it clear that she has a cake which she has made especially and is keen to have your verdict upon it. What are you most likely to do?

19. Can you think of any occasion when the behaviour you expected of yourself as a Christian clashed with what your friends or associates expected of you?

.... Yes
.... No
.... Doubtful

Age Group   .... 18–29 Years   *Occupation:* ....

    30–39

    40–49   ....

    50–59

    60–69   *Sex:*   .... Male

    .... 70 plus   .... Female

Marital Status: .... Married

              .... Single

Note: Questions 1, 10, 13, 15 and 16, were taken from the questionnaire drawn up by G. W. Allport, J. M. Gillespie and J. Young for their study, 'The Religion of the Post-War College Student', *Journal of Psychology*, 25, 1948, pp. 3-33. Before being included in this schedule, however, they have in some cases been subject to considerable alteration.

PUBLISHER'S POSTSCRIPT

PUBLISHER'S POSTSCRIPT

WHEN I first read this book in manuscript I was an incumbent in the Diocese of Birmingham, about to leave my parish for the SCM Press. I did not attempt to identify the four parishes Mr Thompson writes about, and I do not think anything more than idle curiosity would have been satisfied by my doing so. I was convinced that a similar survey of my own parish, or of virtually any other parish of my acquaintance, would yield very similar results. How far Free Churchmen would judge the survey relevant to their circumstances, is not for me to say.

It is possible that Birmingham would make a peculiarly bad showing. The Rev. John Grimwade in a letter to *The Times* on October 17, 1956, produced figures[1] showing that Birmingham has fewer clergy in proportion to the population than any diocese in the country. In so far as the practical absence of the clergy from the lives of the people confuses people about the role of the clergy, some of the points made in chapter IX may be more acutely true in Birmingham than elsewhere because the clergy there are thinner on the ground, and this has probably been true for many decades. But such differences will surely be marginal; for the dominant factors are a more general uncertainty within the Church, and a general disintegration of society.

I myself lacked the time (and possibly also the courage) to apply this approach to my own parish, but though I have prided myself on being a reasonably realistic person, I was clear that had I done so, I should have had a series of salutary shocks.

It may be objected that the conclusions of the survey are negative and unhelpful, and give but little indication of 'where we go from here'. But it was of course no part of the author's academic brief to prescribe remedies, and he would probably, and rightly, hold that it would have been an impertinence for a research student from New Zealand to attempt to do so. He has served us well enough in giving us not the

---

[1] The figures are as follows: Thirty of the 43 English dioceses average one parochial clergyman to 3,000 people or less. Eight have one parish priest for between 3,000 and 5,000 people. The figures for the other five dioceses are: Sheffield, one to 5,100; Southwark, one to 5,450; Liverpool, one to 5,560; London, one to 5,730; Birmingham, one to 6,950.

personal impressions of an individual but the relatively objective findings of a scientific study; and he has wisely explained his methods carefully. Since this is a pioneer work, these may be open to criticism. If, for example, 'the man of great sanctity' in question 8 had been re-phrased 'a really spiritual man', sanctity might have scored more marks. On the other hand his classification of 'occupational status' is preferable to classing almost everyone in an average urban parish as 'artisan'. In these matters the Church is not unlike the patient who says, 'It's me nerves, doctor': in both cases there is much careful detailed factual study to be done before diagnosis and prescription are possible.

I doubt if the positive answers lie ready to hand. This is not to say that they do not exist. They are in the hand of God, and must be sought from Him, in a real desire to know His will for His Church. His will is most likely to be disclosed to congregations who together seek from God His direction for them in the time and place in which He has called them and on which, in acceptance of that calling, they are exercising all the patience and ingenuity that their brains and experience suggest. If *The Church's Understanding of Itself* is in this respect of any service to the Church, author and publisher alike will be more than satisfied.

DAVID M. PATON